A Saint in the Slave Trade

Arnold Lunn

A Saint in the Slave Trade

Peter Claver (1581–1654)

SOPHIA INSTITUTE PRESS
Manchester, New Hampshire

Sophia Institute Press
Box 5284, Manchester, NH 03108
1-800-888-9344

www.SophiaInstitute.com

Sophia Institute Press® is a registered trademark of Sophia Institute.

paperback ISBN 978-1-64413-592-1

ebook ISBN 978-1-64413-593-8

Library of Congress Control Number: 2021948391

First printing

To
Her Royal Highness,
the Infanta Beatrice of Spain

Contents

Part 2
Supplementary Questions

A Saint in the Slave Trade

The Chapter That Became a Book

"Great lovers of mankind such as St. Paul, Augustine, Francis of Assisi, Wesley, and General Booth ..." This sentence from an article in one of the dailies revives old memories. "Lovers of mankind ..." Yes, there was a time when I, too, believed that this was the supreme test, and that saints should be measured by philanthropic standards. Lovers of mankind, or even of animal kind, which is perhaps one of the reasons why St. Francis is such a favorite with English Protestants.

And, provided that the saint loved mankind, it did not matter if he loved them as a Catholic or a Protestant or a Unitarian or a Buddhist, or even as a Rationalist. Was not John Stuart Mill described as "the saint of Rationalism"?

Saints, it seemed, were all much of a muchness.

During my last term at school, I began to read the works of William James and was much impressed by his criticism of Catholic sanctity, which I discovered in his famous book *The Varieties of Religious Experience*. This great work exercised a tremendous influence on the English-speaking world. Its appearance was opportune, for it was published at a moment when Protestantism was deeply infected by defeatism. The odd view that religion and science were in conflict was still widely held. William James staged a magnificent "comeback" to religion after the despondencies of the Darwinian era.

When I was an undergraduate, the universities were infected by the view that dogmatic religion was a survival from a prescientific era, and belief in God was gradually being replaced by a vague respect for an impersonal Absolute. This tenuous abstraction may have protected respectable dons against the charge of vulgar atheism but does not appear to have filled any other function in the universe.

William James was perhaps the first eminent philosopher outside the ranks of official Christian apologists vigorously to reaffirm forgotten truths, such as the existence of God, personal immortality, and free will. He was not an orthodox Christian, for he rejected, among other doctrines, the omnipotence of God, and he nowhere affirms his belief in the divinity of Christ. He was, indeed, a champion of religion in general rather than of any form of religion in particular. "If an Emerson," he wrote, "were forced to be a Wesley, or a Moody forced to be a Whitman, the total of human consciousness of the divine would suffer."

It was this very detachment from official Christianity that made his advocacy of religion so effective, for whereas everybody knows that Christians are biased, few people suspect bias in a latitudinarian. Moreover, James's belief in his own scientific impartiality was infectious. Indeed, he not only preached, but, to some extent, he practiced, the scientific method in his approach to the problems of religion. His approach was inductive rather than deductive, for he spent a vast amount of time collecting data from religious literature, and he made a sincere effort to allow the facts thus collected to speak for themselves.

It was a great achievement to remind philosophers, historians, and scientists that the scientific method that had proved so valuable in science ought to be preferred, even in religion, to the crudity of verdicts based, not on the patient examination of facts, but on a blend of prejudice and ignorance. William James both deserved and achieved success. He gave new courage to timid Christians and was one of the first to disturb the complacency of those who believed that science had dealt a coup de grâce to Christianity, a complacency that has since been completely shattered.

William James was accepted by a generation of Protestants as an authority whose verdict was scientific and impartial. He was, they felt, no fanatic partisan of any particular church. He was biased neither in favor of nor against the Romans and made palpable efforts to be fair to the Roman saints. All of which explains why thousands of Protestants formed their views on Catholic sanctity without opening a single Catholic work or without reading the biography of a single Catholic saint.

His famous chapter on *The Value of Sanctity* is interesting both for what it says and for what it leaves unsaid, for its affirmations, for its omissions, and for its denials. Some of his remarks seem both perverse and shallow to Catholic readers, but an eminent Catholic writer is a little severe when he says that William James, in his chapter on the saints, "never from the outset had the faintest chance of understanding what he was talking about." Fr. de Grandmaison, S.J., who quotes frequently from William James in his book *Personal Religion*, very truly says that William James may well have been "the victim of unskilful hagiography."

Again, it is only fair to remember that William James was the product of a very complacent form of Protestantism. The Catholic Church, as all ill-informed people are aware, takes no interest in social reform. William James, who never alluded to the great papal encyclical *Rerum Novarum*, which has been described as

the Workers' Charter, and who died many years before the pub-
lication of *Quadragesimo Anno*, honestly believed that whereas
Protestantism was progressive and democratic, Catholicism was
reactionary and aristocratic. Like other ardent believers in democracy, he seems unconsciously to have assumed that God, like
a constitutional monarch, must bow to the verdict of the theological electorate. God would change with the changing fashions of
the day. The kind of God that the progressive democrat wanted
was the kind of God that the progressive democrat was going
to get. This, at least, would seem to be the implication of the
following extracts, which I take from his chapter on the saints:
"What with science, idealism, and democracy, our own imagination has now the need of a God of an entirely different temperament.... The God whom mediaeval Catholics worshipped....
Smitten as we are by the vision of social righteousness ... the
best professional sainthood of former centuries seems curiously
shallow and unedifying."

William James was living in the Indian summer of the Liberal-
ism that believed that all international problems could be solved
by the spread of democratic institutions and the universal triumph
of free trade, and no contrast could be greater than the contrast
between the standards of Catholic sanctity and the progressive
Protestantism in which William James believed. James was a
very great man, great enough to triumph, if only partially, over
the provincialism of his background, but it is not surprising that
some of his remarks about the saints are foolish, petulant, and
peevish. What is surprising is the large degree of sympathetic
understanding that he showed for a type of piety so antipathetic
to his own way of thinking.

The impact of Catholic sanctity on great but prejudiced minds
is always interesting. Catholics are not alone in believing *Saint*

Joan to be Mr. Shaw's greatest play, perhaps his only great play. There are passages in this play that suggest that St. Joan all but conquered a foe as stubborn as those against whom she led the cavalry of France, the invincible prejudice of a brilliant but misguided man. And it may well be that it was in a mood of bitter reaction against the truth that he had seen from afar that he wrote that squalid and vulgar tract *The Adventures of the Black Girl in Her Search for God.*

The conflict between truth and prejudice is apparent in the following passages from William James's chapter on the saints.

"I have often thought that in the old monkish poverty-worship, in spite of the pedantry which infested it, there might be something like the moral equivalent of war which we are seeking. When one sees the way in which wealth-getting enters as an ideal into the very bone and marrow of our generation, one wonders whether the belief in poverty as a worthy religious vocation may not be the transformation of 'military courage' and the spiritual reform that our time stands most in need of."

The divided mind is no less obvious in his attitude to the extravagant love of suffering exhibited by so many saints. His first instinct was to diagnose as pathological perversity the insatiable love of suffering exhibited, for instance, by St. Margaret Mary Alacoque. "Nothing but pain," exclaimed this saint, "makes my life supportable." And yet even here intuition triumphed over prejudice. He concludes a noble passage in praise of asceticism with a sentence that no convinced humanist would have written: "The folly of the Cross, so inexplicable to the intellect, has yet its indestructible, vital meaning."

The unwilling tribute of this American humanist is more impressive than the adoration of the convinced Catholic. It would be easy to fill a book with praises of sanctity from Catholic sources, but the Balaam who comes to curse and remains to bless is a more valuable witness than the prophet who needs no conversion.

There are two William Jameses: James the greater, who is beginning to understand "the folly of the Cross," and James the less, who judged the saints by the provincial standards of humanism. James the less was perplexed and perturbed by the attitude of James the greater and, from time to time, reacted with outbursts of petulant provincialism, thus no doubt recapturing the confidence of suspicious readers. Unfortunately, it was not the cautious tribute of James the greater but the impatient criticism of James the less that determined my own youthful attitude to the saints. William James convinced me that few of the Catholic saints would have passed the "lovers of mankind" test. "Smitten as we are," wrote James the less, "by our vision of social righteousness, we feel nothing but an indulgent pity for saints of this type." For saints, in other words, who did little for their neighbors excepting pray for them, which, of course, doesn't count.

Of St. Teresa of Avila, for instance, whom William James describes as "one of the ablest of women," he can only say, "She was tenaciously inspiring, and put her whole life at the service of her religious ideals. Yet so paltry were these to our present way of thinking that (although I know that others have been moved differently) my own feeling in reading her has been pity that so much vitality of soul should have found such poor employment."

Many saints, James writes, fell into "all sorts of holy excesses, fanaticism, self-torment, prudery, scrupulosity, gullibility, and morbid inability to meet the world. By the very intensity of his fidelity to the paltry ideals with which an inferior intellect may inspire him, a saint can be even more objectionable and damnable than a normal man would be in the same situation."

Before I read William James, I believed that there was no real difference between Catholic and Protestant saints, but William James convinced me that Catholic sanctity was ruined by its extravagances. I was faintly disgusted by these revelings in hospital purulence, these self-inflicted penances and superfluities of devotion. Before reading William James, I thought that most saints were much of a muchness, and after reading William James, I came to the conclusion that Catholic saints were too much of a muchness. And in this respect my views remained unchanged for many years. The years passed, but it was not until I started exchanging letters with Fr. Knox that I began to suspect that William James had not said the last word on Catholic sanctity. His influence is still strong in a letter from which the following is an extract:

"Though I admire the ascetic," I wrote, "I am unedified by the kind of self-torture which is common in the lives of Catholic saints. Both suicide and self-torture are extolled in some religions; neither has any place in Christianity. It was the priests of Baal who cut themselves with knives, and I cannot see that the Christian saint is any the better for following their example. One cannot, for instance, imagine Christ wearing a shirt stuffed with jagged nails, or flogging Himself till the blood ran. He died on the Cross without a murmur, but He did not inflict torture on Himself. He did not go out of His way to make Himself uncomfortable, but He was completely indifferent to His comfort—a very different matter. He forgot to eat or sleep when engrossed in prayer, but when 'God sent a cheerful hour' He 'did not refrain.'"

To this, Fr. Knox replied, "You have your own ideas of what the saintly character is, derived from your notions, say, of John Wesley. When a Catholic saint exhibits this character, you say he is no better than John Wesley. When he deviates from it, as, for example, by showing a love of suffering (this is more to the point than the distinction between voluntary and necessary mortifications), you simply comment 'More fool he.'"

It was some time before I began to suspect that Fr. Knox's reply was anything more than a clever debating counterattack. Still, it set me thinking, and my suspicion that Fr. Knox might be right was strengthened by Fr. Martindale's broadcast talks, which are published under the title of *What Are Saints?* Few books have helped me more, and I remember being profoundly impressed by his essay on a man of whom I had never heard, a certain Peter Claver, who worked among the slaves for forty years. Wonderful work, judged even by purely philanthropic standards.

Certainly Claver passed the "lovers of man" test, which was strange, for in other respects he seemed to embody all those aspects of Catholic sanctity that are most obnoxious to our modern humanitarians. He practiced, for instance, the most frightful austerities. An uneasy doubt assailed me. Was there, after all, some obscure link between a hair shirt and philanthropy? Or was the hair shirt merely ridiculous and superfluous? I could not make up my mind, but it was to Claver's philanthropy rather than to his hair shirt that I drew Mr. Joad's attention in a letter in which I tried to persuade him that there was a radical difference between saints like Peter Claver and the noblest of secular humanitarians.

Moreover, I began to realize that the holiness of the Catholic saint has certain sign-marks that differentiate him from the holy men of other religions. These sign-marks are recognizable even by non-Christians, as, for instance, by Henri Bergson, who is a Jew by race, in his brilliant book *Les Deux Sources de la Morale et de la Religion.* The truth is that the man in the street's attitude to religion, "They are all much of a muchness," is as foolish and as superficial as the no-less-unscientific view that there is nothing much to choose between, say, a Catholic saint and a Buddhist monk. It is the resemblances that impress the casual observer, the profound differences that strike the scientific inquirer.

Now what are these hallmarks of sanctity? And in what respect does a saint like St. Peter Claver differ from a good Christian like Mr. Gladstone?

There are certain objective sign-marks of sanctity, such as miracles, which admit of objective proof, but one can no more prove that there is a unique quality in certain types of Catholic saints than one can prove that Shakespeare was a better poet than Kipling.

"I wonder if you would agree with me," wrote Fr. Knox, "that Tennyson, if he had taken opium for six months on end, could never possibly have written *Kubla Khan*? And yet he was a perfectly workmanlike poet. The quality which Coleridge has and he has not is something which you cannot define or analyse; you cannot even prove its existence to a person who does not *feel* it."

One cannot press such analogies too far, and yet analogies from song and art help us to understand the difference between a saint like St. Francis of Assisi and a man of many virtues such as Mr. Gladstone.

The saint, like the artist, is conscious of the universal that informs all particulars. It is, indeed, this sense of the one behind the many that explains the difference between great art and competent workmanship, between the best of the Louvre and the worst of the Luxembourg, between the appeal that is for all time and the trick that catches the passing mood of the day, between Fra Angelico's *Crucifixion*, a window opening onto the timeless realm, and Watts's *Hope*, a mirror reflecting the sentimentalism of Victorian England.

11

A Saint in the Slave Trade

The saints differ, as other people differ, in their human traits but have one characteristic in common—an intense preoccupation with the supernatural. Every sincere Christian is influenced by his belief in the supernatural world, but there are periods in the lives even of the best when this influence wears very thin. This world, with its insistence on petty preoccupations, is too much with us.

> Such harmony is in immortal souls;
> But whilst this muddy vesture of decay
> Doth grossly close it in, we cannot hear it.[1]

The saint wears his "muddy vesture" with a difference and hears the harmony to which grosser ears are deaf. To the ordinary Christian, God is a belief; to the saint, a lover. The saint walks by sight where others walk by faith. He has seen the spirit of God moving on the face of the waters, and from that moment, the common world has been transfigured and the common round transformed.

"It is easy," writes Fr. Knox,

> to pick out points here and there which I should call characteristic of sanctity. As, for instance, the desire of suffering, St. Teresa's *aut pati aut mori*; the notion of vicarious suffering for others, as when St. Ignatius stood in the frozen river to save the libertine; a great simplicity, almost childishness, as when St. John Cantius ran after the highwaymen to tell them that he had some money after all; a deliberate foolishness, like that of St. Philip Neri changing hats with other people to make passersby laugh at him; a fantastic reliance on Providence, like Don Bosco's; a desire to run away, even from a vocation which meant untold

---

[1] William Shakespeare, *The Merchant of Venice*, act 5, scene 1.

good to others, such as that evinced by the Curé d'Ars, and so on. It is quite certain that the ordinary Protestant reader would not be edified by such traits; and indeed some of them are traits which nobody would admire in a man who was not a saint. But, for the sympathetic reader, they show up the medium used for the drawing, which is, I suppose, a completely supernaturalized and, if you will, otherworldly atmosphere. And it is not so much the miracles of the saints which impress me as the fact that, when you read the lives of such people, the miracles seem quite in keeping, quite in the picture; whereas in the biography of any ordinary religious leader—say Bossuet—they would somehow be out of the picture.

A materialist would deny that these characteristics are evidence of the supernatural. Without venturing into a discussion of certain well-attested miracles, we can still provide the materialist with some pretty puzzles on which to exercise his ingenuity. I wonder what he would make of the Curé d'Ars and of the life that he lived. He rose at one in the morning, having retired at midnight, prayed alone in the church, and heard confessions until six. Then he said Mass, and after breakfasting on half a glass of milk, he spent the morning hearing confessions and teaching children. He lunched, standing, on a potato or two, and spent the rest of the day visiting the sick, hearing more confessions, holding his evening service, preaching, and praying. And so to bed, on two planks, at midnight.

He led this life for thirty years, and he died at seventy-three. I call that a miracle in the proper sense of the term, for a life such as this is outside the ordinary course of nature. One hour's sleep in twenty-four, a few potatoes, and an occasional egg does not, believe me, supply the concentrated energy for thirty years of such a life.

And yet the materialist, I suppose, must somehow contrive to persuade himself that energy such as this can be explained in physicochemical terms. He refuses to consider the facts that prove that holiness is a force as real as electricity, for holiness, as Francis Thompson writes, "not merely energizes, not merely quickens; one might almost say it prolongs life." I have taken these words from Francis Thompson's essay *Health and Holiness*, and the passage continues as follows:

> By its Divine reinforcement of the will and the energies, it wrings from the body the uttermost drop of service; so that, if it can postpone dissolution, it averts age, it secures vital vigour to the last. It prolongs that life of the faculties, without which age is the foreshadow of the coming eclipse. These men, in whom is the indwelling of the Author of life, scarce know the meaning of decrepitude: they are constantly familiar with the suffering, but not the palsy, of mortality. Regard Manning, an unfaltering power, a pauseless energy, till the grave gripped him; yet a "bag of bones." That phrase, the reproach of emaciation, is the gibe flung at the saints; but these "bags of bones" have a vitality which sleek worldlings might envy. St. Francis of Assisi is a flame of active love to the end, despite his confessed ill-usage of "Brother Ass," despite emaciation, despite ceaseless labour, despite the daily haemorrhage from his Stigmata. In all these men you witness the same striking spectacle; in all these men, nay, and in all these women. Sex and fragility matter not; these flames burn till the candle is consumed utterly.

A friendly critic who read this book in manuscript criticized me for omitting all reference to those explanations of sanctity in terms of sex that are so popular with the sort of people who have every temptation to explain as many phenomena as possible in terms of the thing that interests them most.

Freud may or may not have contributed something of value to medicine; he has contributed nothing of value to religious philosophy, for Freudianism explains nothing but Freud—a fact that will only surprise those who believe that useful judgments may be expected from people who make no effort whatever to acquire a rudimentary knowledge of the problem under discussion. There is not a page in Freudian literature that betrays any knowledge of Christian philosophy, history, or apologetics.

Laziness is, no doubt, the explanation of Freudianism, since it is much less trouble to psychoanalyze Christians than to master or to meet the arguments for Christianity. Moreover, most Freudians are the victims of a modern superstition, the belief in word-magic. The victims of this illusion really believe that some nasty label, such as masochism, is itself an explanation of the phenomenon that it professes to describe. But you have not explained a phenomenon merely because you have labeled it.[2]

That brilliant adventurer Alcibiades confessed that Socrates alone could inspire him with a feeling of shame.[3] In his presence, he was forced to concede the existence of moral claims that he denied in practice. And so, from time to time, he ran away and wished that Socrates himself would vanish from the world.

---

[2]   I have discussed Freudianism, behaviorism, etc., in three chapters of the new and enlarged edition of *The Flight from Reason*.

[3]   *Symposium*, 216.

A Saint in the Slave Trade

The saint, like Socrates, is an inconvenient reminder of the moral standards we prefer to forget. And the Freudian, like Alcibiades, feels ashamed. But, unlike Alcibiades, he does not run away. He stops—and spits.

Reason brought me to the threshold of the Church, but the final impulse that sent me across the threshold into the sanctuary was provided by Fr. Martindale's *What Are Saints?* All of which I tried to explain in a book that I began to write shortly before I was received. "Tried to," for I did not succeed. The first draft of a chapter about the saints was too long and too superficial. The chapter then developed into two chapters, but with no better results, and finally I cut these chapters out altogether.

The rejected chapter has now developed into a book, for in the pages that follow, I shall try not only to retell the wonderful story of St. Peter Claver's life but also to discuss the more general aspects of this particular type of sanctity.

First, there is the problem of asceticism. St. Peter Claver not only inflicted on his poor body the most appalling penances; he also deprived himself of all the ordinary pleasures of life. Was he right, or were these austerities extravagances that we can at best condone? If, on the other hand, we wholeheartedly admire these extremes of asceticism, must we logically condemn the ordinary Christian who likes his creature comforts? Difficult problems to which there is no easy solution.

"It is perhaps even more difficult," said a distinguished priest in my hearing, "to fit Peter Claver into the Christian scheme than ordinary Christians. Christ, so far as we know, did not wear a hair shirt, and he certainly enjoyed being with normal folk, and indeed was reproved by the Pharisees for eating with publicans and sinners."

The life of Claver raises yet another tremendous issue — the issue of slavery. Claver devoted his life to the slaves, and yet he never, so far as we know, criticized the institution of slavery, which he appears to have taken for granted. He was interested in individuals rather than in institutions, and moreover, so far as slavery is concerned, he would never have condemned an institution that the Church had never explicitly condemned. Was Claver wrong? Was the Church wrong?

Long before I had completed the first draft of this book, I was more than conscious of the immense difficulty of my task. In all questions connected either directly or indirectly with sanctity, the main problem, perhaps, is to preserve that due proportion that you find in all things Catholic.

"Nowhere else," writes Mr. Belloc in his contribution to the symposium *Why I Am and Why I Am Not a Catholic,*

> nowhere else, in all the experience of mankind, will you discover universal Proportion as you discover it in the doctrine of the Catholic Church. Though it applies to the whole of human life, it does, in every relation, keep the normal — which some have translated "the Mean." It does so in the relations of parent and child, or husband and wife, of the propertied man and the destitute, of the citizen and the Christian (I mean of our duty to the Prince and our duty to God). It does so in that most difficult of all actual problems, the management of appetite....
>
> Men have achieved Proportion outside the Faith in one department at the expense of another. They have had the grace given them to satisfy the human spirit to the full in column and arch — and meanwhile to despise justice. They have had exactitude of law, and have meanwhile

despised beauty. They have had a just arrangement of property, and meanwhile have lost culture. But in the Catholic scheme there inhabits a certain balancing compensating spirit, which though it can never constrain men to achieve perfect proportion—for men are fallen—does make them approach to such perfection sufficiently for the right conduct of life.

It is much more difficult for the individual Catholic than for the Church to preserve this sense of proportion, for it is the mission of the Church to correct the excesses of individual Catholics. And in this business of sanctity, it is particularly difficult to retain one's precarious balance on the knife edge of the Catholic mean. Enraged by humanist attacks on asceticism, one drifts into the opposite error. It is easy to forget that, though one may mortify, one must not despise the body. One may sacrifice bodily pleasures, but one must not belittle them. It is precisely because sex is good that celibacy is a worthy offering to the Creator of all good things. Man is both body and soul, and those who begin by despising the body soon slide down the slippery slope that leads to the Manichean heresy.

It is even easier to react to the opposite extreme in angry protest against a certain type of hagiography. It is tempting to insist that the Church has ever been the enemy of Puritanism, easy to preach a heartening sermon on the cheerful text "God does not compete with the good things that He has made and which He has given us. He is to be worshipped through them and in them."

All of which is true, but it is easy to remember that wine and song have their place in the Catholic scheme and easy to forget that asceticism is an integral part of the Christian life. And though it is true that "God does not compete with the good things that He has made," men are frail and only too ready to put God in the second place; and for this reason, we need to be reminded that we are commanded to seek first the Kingdom of God and then, and only then, the other good things may be added.

It is even more difficult to maintain the Catholic balance when discussing the Church's attitude to social problems such as slavery. It is tempting to meet the humanist on his own ground and to accept by implication his view that the Church must be judged solely by her contribution to human happiness in this world. The Church, however, is not a political party that can be criticized for failing to put antislavery into its program, but a transcendental society that was founded to guide men not to Utopia but to Heaven.

But here again we must preserve the Catholic mean and re-member that the Church, though supremely concerned with the salvation of souls, is also concerned to secure the temporal happiness of her children. The great papal encyclicals *Quadrag-esimo Anno* and *Rerum Novarum* deprive Catholics of all excuse for complacently ignoring social evils that should challenge the conscience of all Christian men.

The first part of this book is a biography of St. Peter Claver, and the second part an attempt to discuss some of the "supple-mentary questions" that challenge the student of his life and labors.

I have tried in this book to discuss not sanctity in general but a particular type of saint. There are, so Catholics believe, many saints who are known only to God, for the suburban villa, the shop, and the farm may be nurseries of sanctity no less than the cloister. But clearly, if a saint is known only to God, his particular characteristics form no part of the available evidence on which we form our own tentative, halting notions of sanctity. Then, again, many of the martyr saints were canonized less, perhaps, for any notable difference between their lives and the lives of other good Catholics than for the heroic devotion of their deaths. But the majority of those who have been canonized in recent centuries belong to a very definite type. St. Peter Claver, for instance, and the Curé d'Ars and St. Thérèse of the Child Jesus, to name but a few, were acclaimed by the vox populi long before their holiness was officially recognized by the Church. There is, indeed, a supernatural quality in the lives of such saints that impresses even the most obtuse of their contemporaries. There are, as I have said, saints known only to God, saints whose way of life provokes little comment, friendly or hostile, from their contemporaries, but there are others whose strange behavior is an inspiration to some and a stumbling block to others. It is of such saints that I have *tried* to write in this book.

Yes, "tried to write," for the words with which Ida Coudenhove brings her beautiful study of sanctity to a close will serve my purpose — "*Not*: 'It was thus,' but 'Perhaps the figure of the saint means this too.'"

Part 1

The Life of St. Peter Claver

1

The Man Who Liked Slaves

At the beginning of the seventeenth century, Cartagena, in the Caribbean Sea, was the chief slave market in the New World. The arrival of a new shipload of slaves was the signal for great activity in the port.

Let us watch the slaves as they disembark. Down the gangway they come, a forlorn straggle of hopeless misery, starving, half mad, and frantic with homesickness. They have been chained for three months below decks in an atmosphere so horrible that no white man could thrust his head into it without fainting. They have endured every conceivable form of brutality, physical and mental. Many have died on the voyage, and those who have survived are half dead. They have left everything, home, liberty, families, and have nothing to hope for.

Suddenly the curious crowd of watchers falls back, and a little man bustles through carrying a large basket full of fruit, tobacco, and bandages. His face beams as he approaches the slaves. He wastes no time before getting to work. His first task is to baptize the dying and then to wash and feed the sick. And as he leaves, the slaves crowd round with pathetic demonstrations of affection.

The adoration of the slaves for Fr. Claver was something that was not to be bought with tobacco and fruit. Nor did he win their hearts by attempting to arouse their indignation against their oppressors, for, like other saints, he could love the oppressed without hating the oppressor. He spoke to them not of the wrongs that they had suffered, but of the wrongs that they had inflicted. He tried to provoke tears of contrition for their sins rather than tears of self-pity for their sorrows. Nay, further, he urged upon these slaves the duty of thankfulness for the very sufferings of which they were victims. Supreme audacity! Suffering, he told them, was a blessing and bore the same relation to sin as medicine to disease. "Blessed are they that mourn" was the text from which he preached.

And yet St. Peter Claver was not the forerunner of the type of clergyman, satirized by Bernard Shaw, who urges the poor to "keep their minds on heavenly things and not on trades unions and socialism." Were he living today, he would not be interested in trades unions or socialism. He would have expressed no views on such subjects for the good reason that he would have had no views to express. He was concerned with individuals, not with the social institutions of the day. His life was devoted not to social reform but to the salvation of souls.

Blessed are they that mourn, blessed are they that suffer every malignity that man can inflict, for these bodily sufferings can be the instrument for the emancipation from sin. The world, St. Peter Claver continued, could offer them nothing. No remission and no relief from their fetters. But in the world to come he could promise them the glorious freedom of the sons of God.

These remarks were not received with catcalls and bricks, nor was the absence of hostile demonstration due to the fact that the slaves were too cowed to voice their indignant disapproval. On the contrary, they crowded round St. Peter Claver and begged him to come again. And he came again. And continued coming for some forty years. I wonder how many of our modern humanitarians would have won their adoring love. I wonder whether these slaves would have encored Mr. Bertrand Russell had he favored them with a reading from his book *The Conquest of Happiness*.

The modern social reformers, had they been translated in time to Cartagena, would have sympathized strongly with the slaves and might have devised admirable schemes for educating them and raising their social status. They would have found it far less easy to simulate affection for them as individuals. You see, in the first place, they stank, and it is so difficult to love people who stink.

Fr. Claver, however, had not the least difficulty in making them believe that he had been hanging round the harbor for hours so as not to waste a precious moment in making their acquaintance. The first sight of the slave ship had given him much the same thrill as a ship bearing a bride gives to the bridegroom waiting in the harbor. He made them believe all this because he believed it himself.

Nor did he confine himself to expressions of personal affection. He told them of one whose love for them was infinite and whose compassion was unbounded. He spoke with such conviction that the miracle for which he prayed never failed to happen. The poor outcasts fell on their knees and, through a mist of tears, worshipped the God who had made the slave trader in His image, the God of the white man who had torn them from their homes, the God of the brutes who had treated them as brutes. God was all this, but He was also the God of Fr. Claver.

Fr. Claver accepted slavery as an integral part of the social system; it was the slave, not slavery, whom he wished to reform. Reformers may broadly be classified into those who try to change the man and those who try to change the institution. Claver, as we have seen, was concerned only with the man. This was his vocation, and there are other vocations, for the slow betterment of the world is due not only to the Clavers who love slaves but also to the Wilberforces who hate slavery.

The modern world is in no danger of underestimating the importance of improving a man's environment, for we are all busily engaged in building the New Jerusalem with marketing boards, slum clearances, and five-year plans. Our difficulty is to remember that the State exists for individuals, not individuals for the State, and our temptation is to lose sight of the individual against the background of mass averages and health statistics. And for this reason, among many others, St. Peter Claver has a special message for the modern world.

2

Claver's Early Life

St. Peter Claver was born about 1581, some say 1583, at Verdu in the Diocese of Solfona in the principality of Catalonia. Philip II was on the throne of Spain and Sixtus V on the throne of St. Peter.

Peter Claver's parents belonged to families of distinguished and ancient lineage, and, like many other Spaniards of impeccable ancestry, they were far from rich. Their poverty troubled them not at all. They were pious without ostentation, devoted to each other, and no less devoted to their only son. In this devout and harmonious atmosphere, the young Peter Claver grew to manhood.

St. Peter Claver's life was set from the first in the path of holiness and directed with unerring aim, *sicut sagitta a sagittante*, to the target of sanctity. His mother, influenced, so we are told, by an ambition to imitate the two women whose name she bore, Anne the mother of Samuel and Anne the mother of Mary, devoted her son to the priesthood in her mind while he was yet a child. To her great joy, she noted that he displayed from the first a great love for the service of the altar.

Piety offends only when it implies a censorious verdict on the impious, for it is preachiness, not preaching, that most people resent. The saint is as impersonal in his condemnation of sin as he is personal in his love of God. He can praise holiness without appearing to praise himself. He can attack sin without seeming to attack the sinner. He has mastered the fine art of conversion, the technique of setting Christ on a pedestal while himself remaining firmly anchored to the ground. The saint speaks to the sinner on the sinner's level and does not talk down to him from the heights.

Peter Claver graduated with distinction from the Jesuit College of Barcelona. When he was admitted to his degree, the bishop himself, before conferring the tonsure and the four minor orders, paid a marked tribute to his character and his learning, a tribute that filled Peter Claver with acute embarrassment and dismay.

After receiving the tonsure, Claver was possessed by a great longing to join the Society of Jesus, but his humility acted as a brake on his ambition. He felt that he was unworthy of so great an honor, and it was only after considerable delay that he dared to broach the subject to his confessor. His confessor encouraged him to apply to his superiors, who acceded to his wishes but delayed definite acceptance of his proposal until they had had an opportunity, in accordance with the wise provisions of the order, of watching him closely for some months. At the end of this period, they told him that his wish would be granted, provided that he first obtained his parents' consent.

This request was painful to his parents. They had entrusted his education to the Jesuits in order to prepare him for an honorable and distinguished career in the Church and had not reckoned upon the possibility that contact with the Jesuits might lead him into the order itself. To his parents, the difference was crucial. As a secular priest, he would have lived in their world and would probably have succeeded in due course to the wealthy and important canonry held by his uncle. However little such worldly ambition may have weighed with them, they would have been inhuman had they not preferred for their son a career that would not have severed the links between them. As a Jesuit, he would inevitably lose touch with his parents, for his whole life would be centered in the community of which he was a member. It is to their lasting credit that they made no attempt to dissuade him. They accepted the sacrifice in no ungrudging spirit.

He entered the novitiate at Tarragona in his twentieth year. When he entered the cell that had been allotted to him, he was exalted by a transport of delight.

It is easier to attain than to remain on the heights, but the edge of Claver's supernatural happiness was never blunted. His affectionate humility, which had endeared him to his superiors during his novitiate, never lost its freshness. He remained completely unconscious of any change in his position. Fr. Provincial Gaspard, who had been a novice with him, saw him after a long interval of years at Cartagena. "I here find Fr. Claver," he wrote, "as much a novice as when I knew him at Tarragona."

It is the custom of the Society of Jesus that novices should make a pilgrimage to some place of devotion in memory of the pilgrimage that St. Ignatius made to Our Lady of Montserrat immediately after his conversion. Claver was delighted that the pilgrimage that had been assigned to him was none other than Montserrat itself. He set out accordingly with two companions, without food and without money, under instruction to live by charity and to lodge as much as possible in the hospitals. There are many pleasanter ways of traveling than begging alms from door to door. St. Peter Claver was charmed, for if a door slammed in his face, his love of suffering was gratified, and if generous alms were forthcoming, he was the richer by money, most of which could be given away again to the poor. That is the best of being a saint. If things go well, he is pleased, and if things go ill, he is delighted.

The young novices passed three days at Montserrat, days the greater part of which were spent before the shrine of Our Lady. Claver fell in love with Montserrat and would willingly have spent there the remainder of his life, and though he was never to see Montserrat again, in the years that were to come he could never hear the name without profound emotion. In the words of an early chronicler, "Obedience alone withdrew him from that sacred spot, but he left his heart there."

3

The Tempering of the Steel

Peter Claver entered his novitiate on August 7, 1602, and took his final vows on August 8, 1604.

To the modern humanist, the life that St. Peter lived during his novitiate may well seem to have consisted in nothing more than a futile routine of prayers and penances, a routine expressly designed to subordinate the will and to mold the personality for corporate ends. Neither the means employed nor the end achieved appeal to the humanitarian, yet an intelligent humanist who is not completely blinded by prejudice might concede, as William James conceded, that the fine fruits of this training are most impressive. The Spiritual Exercises of St. Ignatius proved their worth in the most exacting of all tests, the test of the rack. In the torture chamber of the Tower, the steel forged in this process did not snap.

On one great point, obedience, the modern world is less unsympathetic to the Jesuit ideals than the world in which William James lived. Over great areas of the modern world an obedience far blinder than any that St. Ignatius demanded is enforced under pain of death, imprisonment, or banishment. There is, indeed, a curiously old-fashioned flavor about the passage in which William James announces his heroic effort to understand the strange virtue of obedience. "First of Obedience," he writes:

> The secular life of our twentieth century opens with this virtue held in no high esteem. The duty of the individual to determine his own conduct and profit or suffer by the consequences seems, on the contrary, to be one of our best-rooted contemporary Protestant social ideals. So much so that it is difficult even imaginatively to comprehend how men possessed of an inner life of their own could ever have come to think the subjection of its will to that of other finite creatures recommendable. I confess that to myself it seems something of a mystery. Yet it evidently corresponds to a profound interior need of many persons, and we must do our best to understand it.

The individualism that William James considered to be the "best-rooted of Protestant ideals" has been uprooted in the very country that claims to be the birthplace of Protestantism. The Church, which was once attacked for its insistence on obedience, is today criticized in many states because it champions freedom. The Church is a divine mean, and secular fashions always oscillate between violent extremes. In a world drunk with the sophistries of Rousseau, the Church was hated as the enemy of liberty, equality, and fraternity, but when license, inequality, and class warfare sent the pendulum swinging back toward tyranny, the Church was regarded with distrust as the disintegrating focus for those who believe in liberty. To the disciples of Rousseau the Church said, "Yes, liberty is good, but there is also a place in life for authority." To the new authoritarians the Church says, "Yes, authority is good, but there is also a place in life for liberty."

The Ignatian insistence on obedience that both shocked and startled William James may shock, but has lost its power to surprise, the modern reader. There is indeed a very modern touch in the passage in which an early biographer summarizes the views of St. Ignatius on obedience.

"I ought," Bartoli-Michel reports St. Ignatius as saying,

on entering religion, and thereafter, to place myself entirely in the hands of God, and of him who takes His place by His authority. I ought to desire that my Superior should oblige me to give up my own judgment, and conquer my own mind.... In the hands of my Superior, I must be as soft wax, a thing, from which he is to require whatever pleases him, be it to write or receive letters, to speak or not to speak to such a person, or the like; and I must put all my fervor in executing zealously and exactly what I am ordered. I must consider myself as a corpse which has neither intelligence nor will; be like a mass of matter which without resistance lets itself be placed wherever it may please anyone; like a stick in the hand of an old man, who uses it according to his needs and places it where it suits him. So must I be under the hands of the Order, to serve it in the way it judges most useful.

I must never ask of the Superior to be sent to a particular place, to be employed in a particular duty.... I must consider nothing as belonging to me personally, and as regards the things I use, be like a statue which lets itself be stripped and never opposes resistance.

St. Ignatius, of course, was only emphasizing a virtue that has always been held in high esteem in the Catholic Church, and which is necessarily regarded as the foundation of monastic life. Indeed, the famous phrase "corpselike obedience" (*perinde ac cadaver*) seems to have been first used by a saint whom few moderns associate with authoritarianism, for it was St. Francis of Assisi who insisted that a brother must regard himself "like as a corpse which receives light and spirit from the Spirit of God by harbouring obediently the will of God."

The principle of obedience is, then, common to all religious orders, but the great emphasis of the Jesuits on this virtue is due to the fact that the Society of Jesus has always been regarded as an army that establishes close contact with the enemy. The Jesuit, precisely insofar as he mixes freely with the world, is exposed to greater temptations and must be protected by severer discipline. Furthermore, the Jesuits, in conducting their campaign in the most remote corners of the globe, would not have achieved the successes that they have achieved had they not been linked with one another under the central directing power of the order by a discipline of iron.

Unity of command was forced on the Allies in the Great War by the pressure of facts, and unity of command was no less essential in the campaign in which St. Ignatius engaged.

Catholics are not alone in using military metaphors, for Protestant preachers very rightly insist on the fact that the Church is at war. But there is a certain inconsistency in singing with enthusiasm hymns such as "Onward, Christian Soldiers" and condemning as tyrannical the discipline and obedience that are as necessary in spiritual as in secular warfare.

Loyola, who could appreciate as the result of personal experience the value of military discipline, for he had served as an officer in the Spanish army and had been converted while recovering from the effects of a leg broken by a cannonball, fully intended that the General of his Society should possess powers similar to those of the generals under whom he had served. The government of friaries and monasteries is normally left to the individual chapters, but the General of the Society of Jesus, theoretically at least, appoints and dismisses officers at will and is responsible only to the general congregation, who can summon him if he is charged with serious offenses.

The famous metaphors that St. Ignatius used must not be pressed too far. It was from the earlier ascetical writings that he borrowed such phrases as "the blind man," "the corpse," and "the old man's staff." He was anxious to drive home his point with vivid imagery. But, in actual fact, the obedience of the Jesuits is far less unqualified than the obedience expected of subordinates in an army. It is a matter of routine in an army for superior officers to make reports on their subordinates, but subordinates are not encouraged to report on their superiors. St. Ignatius fully realized that cases would arise when a superior's order might appear impracticable, unreasonable, and unrighteous to a free subject. It might indeed be so. "In such cases," writes Fr. Pollen, "it is the acknowledged duty of the subject to appeal, and his judgment as well as his conscience, even when it may happen to be ill-informed, is to be respected; provision is made in the Constitution for the clearing up of such troubles by discussion and arbitration, a provision which would be inconceivable, unless a mind and a free will, independent of and possibly opposed to that of the superior, were recognised and respected."

And in this connection it may be as well to remind the reader that the famous maxim "The end justifies the means," popularly attributed to the Jesuits, finds no place in any of their works. The Catholic Church has never compromised on this issue. In no circumstances is it right to sin, and exhortations to obedience are always qualified by the reservation, explicitly stated or implied, that obedience must never be pleaded as an excuse for sin. "Time and again," as Fr. Pollen points out, "those who impute to the Jesuits as a body, or to any of their publications, the use of this maxim to justify evil of any sort have been asked to cite one single instance of such usage, but all to no purpose."

In 1905, for instance, this question came before the civil courts of Trier and Cologne, but the signal failure of Hoensbroech to cite any such example of Jesuit teaching had no more effect than previous refutations. The legend still persists, for no fire is needed to provide the smoke of calumny.

The obedience upon which St. Ignatius insists is an obedience dedicated solely to the glory of God and developed very largely by the famous Spiritual Exercises of St. Ignatius. Two things are necessary for the development of sanctity: grace and the response of the human will. God draws, but man must respond. The realization that the human will plays its part was no Ignatian novelty. St. Ignatius, in stressing the importance of the human will, emphasized an accepted truth. "I can find God," he declared, "whenever I will." And he impressed upon his Society his own conviction that just as the body can be developed by physical exercises, so spirituality can be developed by spiritual exercises.

His Spiritual Exercises were intended to provide a method of self-government and self-conquest. All desires and all actions must be subordinated to the principal object of life, an object that St. Ignatius summed up in the words "I am created to praise God in word and deed and to save my soul."

The purpose of the Ignatian exercises is defined to be that we should make ourselves indifferent toward created things, not desiring health more than sickness, riches more than poverty, honor from men more than their contempt, but only wishing for and desiring that which will best help us to fulfill the true purpose of life.

Here a word of caution is necessary, for so many commentators have been misled by the word *indifferent*. The "indifference in regard to all created things" that St. Ignatius urged upon all his followers was not the indifference of the unemotional but the complete control of emotion no less powerful because disciplined. St. Ignatius desired that his followers should use rather than quench their emotions but should use them in the right way. The Jesuit was not to be at the mercy of his emotions. They were to be like hounds on a leash, released only at the will of their master.

By *indifference*, St. Ignatius meant a habit of mind that is not at the mercy of every suggestion and attraction, a quiet poise that is very different from mechanical stiffness.

Great stress is laid on the imagination, which is constantly invoked to clothe the idea with a visible form. The exercitant is instructed to make every effort to picture to himself the synagogues, villages, and towns through which Christ passed. He is, for instance, to ask himself whether the road leading from Nazareth to Bethlehem is flat or whether it leads through valleys or over heights, to picture to himself the cave of the Nativity, how broad or how narrow, how low or how lofty, and how constructed. He is in imagination to taste the loaves and fishes with which Jesus fed the multitude, to smell the ointment with which St. Mary Magdalen anointed the feet of Christ, and to endure the torture of the Cross.

Many non-Catholic commentators have been misled by such passages and have failed to realize that images play only an incidental role in these exercises, which are primarily designed to appeal not only to the senses but to the mind, heart, and reason.

A Saint in the Slave Trade

After making his disciples see clearly the end and meaning of life and the folly, even on purely natural and rational grounds, of choosing that which can only make a shipwreck of ultimate happiness, St. Ignatius exalts imagination and reason by love. He gives a key meditation on the Kingdom of Christ and one on the two standards, a series of meditations on the life of Christ. He wishes reason to have a guide who is King and Lover. So love takes up the argument, and the exercitant begins to want to imitate Christ in poverty rather than riches, humility rather than pride. This is the secret of St. Francis Xavier's passion and the giving of himself for love by St. Peter Claver.

The Spiritual Exercises, either in their original or in a modified form, have provided the basis of thousands of retreats both within and without the Society of Jesus. "The importance of St. Ignatius's book," wrote Leo XIII in his Brief of February 8, 1900, "with regard to the eternal welfare of souls has been proved by an experience of three centuries and by the evidence of those remarkable men who during this lapse of time have distinguished themselves in the ascetic paths of life or in the practice of sanctity."

4

"And Cannot Come Again"

After completing his novitiate at Tarragona, Fr. Claver was sent by his superiors first to the college of Girone and, a little later, to Palma in Majorca, where the Jesuit college of Montesione had been recently founded.

Claver had the makings of a great scholar, and as he had the gift of passing on his knowledge to others, his services as a teacher were highly valued. He was also no mean dialectician, and he was, in consequence, appointed to plead in one of the public debates that took place from time to time. He accepted this position with the mortification that he invariably showed when he was singled out for any distinction, and his mortification was increased when he was congratulated on acquitting himself in a manner that reflected glory on his college.

At Montesione, Claver met the man who was destined, under God, to give concrete shape to his spiritual ambitions. Alonso Rodriguez had inherited a small business and had lived the life of a businessman until he was forty. His wife and children being then dead, he entered the Society of Jesus and was appointed the gatekeeper at the College of Montesione, holding this post for over twenty years. In his old age, he was reduced to the position of assistant at the gate. This was the position that he held when, at the age of seventy-two, he first met Claver.

There is a charming passage on Alonso in Fr. Martindale's book *Captains of Christ*. "Alonso had achieved," writes Fr. Martindale,

an astonishing degree of sanctity — sanctity, however, of a type singularly baffling to those who measure the worth of human qualities by common sense alone, and regard a life commensurate with the visible scheme of things as an adequate expression of spiritual possibilities. Alonso, even to the "average religious man" of today, though not of his own day, is something of a stumbling-block; to the Greeks among us he is sheer foolishness. The incredible naïveness with which he translated his theories of abnega-tion into act issues into anecdotes exasperating to all who cannot take these incidents, in the concrete, as it were, incorporate with this man, this lay-brother, who made himself loved by all, and honoured, instinctively, not only by all Majorca, but by many hundreds on the mainland, whither his fame had reached; men who, "in a veritable second childhood of religion", were wise to discern the hero. It may be that old men of this type — I will not say, the complete expression of the type, like Alonso — are not so seldom to be met with in the ranks of lay-brothers of religious Orders. Perhaps anyone who has lived in a larger house of some such Order — a house of studies, for example — will remember more than one of these gentle old men, full of profound spiritual insight expressing itself often in acts of the most pathetic childlikeness or downright childishness. And such encounters come, I would dare to say, with a sweetness singularly refreshing to a mind in danger of sophistication, for the moment, by too much metaphysic or jaded, at any rate, by intellectual drudgeries. *Non in dialectica.*... Let so much, then, be said in homage of Alonso, and in affectionate recollection of not a few of his brothers, still, or not long since, among us.

The closest of friendships was soon formed between this lovable old porter and the devoted young man. Rodriguez, as Miss Petre finely says, found in Claver "the son of his spiritual longings, the disciple who could preach to those for whom he had prayed; who could actually labour among those for whom he had wept and suffered."

St. Peter Claver's superiors were so pleased with this friendship that they arranged a special time in the day when the two could meet and converse without interference in their duties. One day, as Peter Claver passed out of the gate with a companion, Alonso said to him, "Remember, the three adorable Persons of the Blessed Trinity accompany you." These words cast St. Peter Claver into an ecstasy, one of those ecstasies that are frequent in the lives of very holy people, and which it is the habit of our clever modern thinkers to compare with mediumistic trances.

One night, Alonso was transported in a vision to the abode of the blessed and was shown by his guardian angel twelve glorious thrones, one of which was vacant. "This throne," said the angel, "is for thy disciple, Claver. It is the recompense of his virtues and of the great number of souls he will gain to God in the West Indies." Alonso said nothing at the time, but when the moment was approaching for Peter Claver's departure, he drew him aside and said, "I cannot express to you the sorrow that I feel at seeing that God is unknown to the greater part of the world, owing to the scarcity of priests who go to preach His name.... We see many useless workmen where there is no harvest, and where the harvest is abundant there are so few workmen. How many souls in America might be sent to Heaven by priests who are idle in Europe. The riches of those countries are prized, whilst the people are despised. Savage as these men may seem, they are diamonds, unpolished, it is true, but whose beauty will repay the lapidary's skill. If the glory of God's house concerns you, go to the Indies and save millions of these perishing souls. To be willing to go under obedience is certainly much, but not enough for a Jesuit. That being his first and most noble vocation, he should signify his eagerness for it to his superiors, and earnestly solicit such a function. Represent your own desires immediately to them; beg, urge, entreat of them to send you: reiterated entreaties are not contrary to obedience when there is reason to believe that the superior demurs only to try our constancy."[4]

Peter Claver lost no time in following this advice. He wrote to his Superior and was informed that his vocation would be examined when he arrived at Barcelona, whither he was to proceed for the study of theology. Alonso parted with deep sorrow from his young friend and gave him the gift that Claver was to treasure all his life: a few papers containing some of his reflections on the religious life. Here are some extracts:

A religious who would advance in virtue must study to know himself: knowing himself, he will despise himself; but not knowing himself, he becomes proud. He must speak little with men, and much with God. When he

---

[4] Bertrand Gabriel Fleuriau and Luigi Berlendis, *The Life of the Venerable Father Claver, S.J., Apostle of the West Indies: And Memoirs of the Religious Life of Cardinal Odescalchi, S.J.* (London: T. Richardson and Son, 1849), 24–25.

speaks, let him always speak well of others, and as far as possible, ill of himself. He ought, like Melchisedech, to be without father, mother, or relatives; because he must look upon them as not belonging to him: God alone must hold the place of all to him. Let him not regard matters of curiosity, or hearken to useless news, which only cause distractions.

Peter Claver himself, at this time, drew up some maxims for his own use, among others a few striking sentences on the subject of obedience. "Let a man prefer nothing to obedience, no matter who commands.... If he cannot do all, and is asked the reason, let him be content with simply saying that he could not; and for the rest to all that may be said, let him answer nothing—no, absolutely nothing: whatever reproaches may be made, let him be silent, accepting all for the sake of God; provided it be nothing contrary to God, or contrary to obedience. This is indeed the way to vanquish self."

In due course, Peter Claver was ordered to proceed to Barcelona. Claver's companions did not like the look of the ship in which they were to sail. They decided to wait until they could find a more seaworthy vessel. Claver, however, showed trust in God, embarked at once, and arrived safely at Barcelona. His companions were less fortunate, for the ship in which they eventually sailed was captured by Barbary pirates, and they themselves were sold as slaves.

Soon after his arrival at Barcelona, Peter Claver repeated his request to be sent to the Indies. His superiors were anxious to test his resolution, and they were perhaps also influenced by their reluctance to lose a young man of such promise from their province. Peter Claver was accordingly kept for two years at

Barcelona, studying and teaching theology, before his request was finally granted by the Provincial Father.

Claver kept the letter appointing him to his mission until he died. Throughout his life, he often reread it to recapture the joy and ecstasy that he had experienced on first receiving this passport to a life of unending hardship and unremitting toil.

The road to Seville, and thence to the harbor from which he was to sail to the Indies, led him to a crossways within two miles of his home. Field and flower were fragrant with the loveliness of the southern spring as he passed slowly along a road that carried the strong imprint of boyish memories. Two miles separated him from the father he loved and from the mother who had dedicated him while yet in the cradle to the service of the altar. He knew that he was leaving them forever, that there could be no returning down the path that he was to travel across the "salt estranging sea."

> Into my heart the air that kills
> From yon far country blows:
> What are those blue remembered hills,
> What spires, what farms are those?
>
> That is the land of lost content,
> I see it shining plain.
> The happy highways where I went,
> And cannot come again.[5]

And here was the old crossroads. How well he knew it. The road ahead led to Seville, the right-hand road to his home.

---

[5] A. E. Housman, "A Shropshire Lad."

He hesitated, and fumbled, and pulled out a little book and read the words that the saintly old porter had used so often: "He ought, like Melchisedech, to be without father, mother, or relatives; because he must look upon them as not belonging to him: God alone must hold the place of all to him."

The place of all ... Why, yes, of course. And so the new Melchisedech gives a sad shrug to his shoulders, brushes something away from his eyes, and takes the high road for Seville. For four and forty years, he was to spend and be spent in the service of the most wretched of all the sons of Adam. He did what he did, not to store up merit in Heaven but because he was consumed by love for the outcasts among whom he worked. He was to suck the poison from the ulcerous sores of slaves whose very stench appalled all but the stoutest heart, because he knew that a slave is made in the image of God, and because he accepted this truth not as a cold statement of academic fact but as a glorious discovery that never lost its freshness. At a great price, he had attained this divine compassion; the love that defied every natural instinct had been bought by the sacrifice of that love that every natural instinct reinforces. The slave of the slaves was not free to love the free.

God does ask a lot from his elect.

Sanctity escapes our poor human measures. We need neither condemn nor condone actions so offensive to the modern humanitarian. We need not even try to understand. Had we been there when St. Peter took the Seville road, we should have knelt as he passed, and we can still kneel.

5

The Church and Slavery

The silences of the Church have irritated many an ardent social reformer. The identification of "practical Christianity" with the progressive policy of the moment would have been much easier if Christ had only been more explicit on such problems as war, slavery, or the rights of women.

Christ, who was a citizen of a conquered country, never talked about self-determination or the rights of minorities. Almost His only reference to the problem of the relation between the individual and the State under which he lives was the enigmatical command "Render unto Caesar the things that are Caesar's," enigmatical since the controversy between Caesar and his subjects always turns on the delicate point as to precisely what things are Caesar's.

The Church is attacked when it speaks, and the Church is attacked for failing to speak. Christ said nothing about the Immaculate Conception, and therefore the Church is wrong to have made a pronouncement on this subject. Christ said nothing about slavery, and therefore the Church is wrong to have delayed a pronouncement on this subject. The King can do no wrong. The Church can do no right.

A Saint in the Slave Trade

The first draft of this chapter was submitted to a non-Catholic critic, who covered the margin with bitter protests. "Why didn't your infallible Church stop slavery? Surely the infallible Church ought to have known that slavery was wrong.... The Church could have stopped the slave trade had she wanted to."

I sighed gently when I read these comments. Though industrious by force of circumstance, I am idle by temperament, and I foresaw that it would be useless to discuss the relation of the Church to slavery until I had written several pages in the vain hope of making clear to my critic, and to readers of his way of thinking, that there is a very real distinction between an infallible Church and a Delphic oracle.

At such moments, one cannot help wishing that theologians had made matters easier for the faithful by a nicer choice of words. A learned theologian once said to me that much trouble would have been saved if the word *inerrancy* were substituted for the word *infallibility*, for it is not only the ignorant but also those who have more learning than judgment who habitually confuse infallibility with omniscience and assume that an infallible pope could reasonably be expected to provide, on demand, the correct reply to any question on faith or morals.

Dr. Coulton, for instance, in his book on infallibility, points out with triumph that the divine inspiration of the book of Tobit was only settled by the Council of Trent in the sixteenth century. "But nothing could have been easier," he exclaims, "than for an infallible pope to tell Christendom once and for all which books could be relied upon and which could not for inerrancy."

And, of course, if papal infallibility were all that ill-informed critics believe it to be, the pope could no doubt have told us all about Tobit and lots of other things. But a guarantee that the Church will not mislead is not the same as a guarantee that the

Church will invariably give a lead. The pope is protected from giving a wrong answer, but he is not necessarily inspired to give the right answer. He may decline to answer at all. The Church is protected from teaching error, but the Church is left to find out many things for itself. An infallible Church is by no means the same thing as an omniscient Church.

God gave us our brains to use, and revelation was never intended as a labor-saving device. Every Catholic from the pope downward prays for guidance and is expected to employ his faculties to the best advantage in the search for truth.

Revelation provides a broad outline of the Christian life, but God has left us to fill in many details for ourselves. In some cases, God has laid down general principles, but experience alone enables the Church to apply those general principles to particular cases. Murder is a sin, but are hangmen or soldiers guilty of murder? The Church has always answered this question with an unhesitating negative.

If slavery and warfare were sinful *per se* rather than *per accidens*, they might well have been forbidden as definitely and as dogmatically as murder, stealing, and adultery have been forbidden.

Christians today agree in wholeheartedly condemning slavery, and in cooperating in the cause of peace, because experience has proved that the safeguards with which the Church attempted to humanize the institution of slavery proved impracticable, and because the overwhelming majority of wars violate those conditions of a just war as defined by the Church.

The statement that slavery is not necessarily incompatible with Christianity will provoke the indignation of the non-Catholic reader, for few people realize today the radical distinction between the pagan slavery, which the Church condemned, and the Christian form of slavery, which the Church was prepared to condone. There was, for instance, a vastly greater difference between the status of the slave of a pagan and the slave of a conscientious Christian than between a medieval serf and a Victorian farm laborer. The pagan conception of slavery implied complete dominion over the slave. The master had no obligations to the slave, and the slave had no rights. The master was permitted to flog, to torture, to kill or seduce his slaves at will. The slave, on his side, was free neither to choose his religion nor to marry against his master's wishes. He was a living chattel and nothing more. Pagan slavery was utterly irreconcilable with the Christian doctrine of the infinite value of every human soul.

The Church from the first insisted that the slave had rights of which he could not be deprived and that the master had obligations to the slave. Christianity, indeed, by its emphasis on individual responsibility, improved the status of the slave and rendered more sensitive the conscience of the master. It will be convenient to distinguish these two conceptions of slavery by the terms *Christian slavery* and *pagan slavery*, respectively.

Christian slavery can be described as a compulsory contract in accordance with which the slave places his time and the result of his labor at the disposal of his master. But though the slave's working time is at the complete disposal of his master, the slave himself retains the inalienable rights of which no man may be deprived.

These rights the great theologian Cardinal John De Lugo (1583–1660) defined to be as follows: The slave retains his right to his life, to his body and limbs, and to his reputation. In these respects he is to be considered by his master not as a slave but as a man, and his master is bound to make restitution to him for any wrong on these points, just as if he were a free man. A slave who has good reason to fear death or mutilation may lawfully fly, and so may also a female slave who has been solicited by her master to sin. De Lugo also insists that slaves cannot be prohibited by their master from marrying, for marriage is to be reckoned among the goods of the body.

"Slavery," writes De Lugo, "consists in this, that a man is obliged, for his whole life, to devote his labour and services to a master. Now as anybody may justly bind himself, for the sake of some anticipated reward, to give his entire services to a master for a year, and he would in justice be bound to fulfill this contract, why may not he bind himself in like manner for a longer period, even for his entire lifetime, an obligation which would constitute slavery?"[6]

The next quotation is from the last Catholic theologian who defines the limits within which slavery can be legitimately defended. Cardinal Gerdil (1718–1802) writes as follows:

> Slavery is not to be understood as conferring on one man the same power over another that men have over cattle. Wherefore they erred who in former times refused to include slaves among persons; and believed that however barbarously the master treated his slave he did not violate any right of the slave. For slavery does not abolish the natural equality of men: hence by slavery one man is understood to become subject to the dominion of another to the extent that the master has a perpetual right to all those services which one man may justly perform for another; and subject to the condition that the master shall take due care of his slave and treat him humanely.[7]

---

[6] *De Justitia et Jure*, disp. VI, sec. 2, no. 14.
[7] *Comp. Instit. Civil.*, L., vii.

The four titles to lawful slavery were considered by theologians to be:
1. The right of just war.
2. Condemnation for crime.
3. Sale of a man by himself, or, under grave restrictions, of children by their father.
4. Birth of slave mother.

According to the medieval *Jus Gentium* (law of nations), a prisoner of war might lawfully be put to death. Most prisoners of war, then as now, would have preferred slavery to death, and consequently a man who might justly have been executed might justly be enslaved.

The modern *Jus Gentium* no longer recognizes the lawfulness of executing prisoners, but spies may lawfully be executed, and most spies would cheerfully accept enslavement as an alternative to a firing squad.

The second title of lawful slavery is still universally recognized. Slavery is a recognized punishment for the commission of crime. It is clear that life imprisonment is an aggravated form of slavery, for under most penal systems, a prisoner is deprived of many natural rights. The prisoner is far less free than a slave, for the prisoner is deprived of many natural rights that the slave enjoys, such as the right to marriage.

No modern theologian would dream of defending the third and fourth titles of lawful slavery. It is, however, well to remind ourselves that slavery in a modified form is far more common in the modern world than is commonly supposed. If we accept De Lugo's view that slavery consists in this, that the slave is obliged for his whole life to give his entire services to his master, a man who is obliged to devote his entire services to a master for a limited period, or part of his services to his master for all his life, may be regarded as either being wholly enslaved for a limited time or partially enslaved for his whole life.

The essence of slavery surely consists in two conditions. First, that a man is compelled to work for a given master, and secondly, that he is not free to terminate his engagement with the master in question.

Now, payment of taxes represents, in effect, compulsion to devote the entire results of one's labor to the government for a particular portion of the year. The man who pays five shillings in the pound in income tax is, in effect, compelled to work for the government for three months in the year. This is not slavery so long as he is free to elect and to dismiss the government, but the taxpayer in a country where there is no freedom of election is compelled to work for the government for a fraction of the year, and has no power of terminating the engagement. His condition, therefore, approximates, in this respect at least, to that of a slave. Moreover, there are today in modern Europe millions of men who have been transferred from the rule of their compatriots to the government of their conquerors. Such men are compelled to work for a master who is not of their choosing, and they are not free to terminate the engagement at will. Again, it is clear that a man who is forced to serve as a conscript in the army of a country that has conquered the country of his birth, is, in effect, a slave at least for the period of his military service.

There are, of course, hundreds of thousands of men in modern Europe who are subjected to forced labor or interned in concentration camps because their political views differ from the views of those in authority. Such men are deprived of many of the natural rights that the Church endeavored to secure for the slave.

Indeed, the slave who was owned by a conscientious Christian, who obeyed both the letter and the spirit of the Church's teaching in the relation of the slave owner to the slave, might, in some respects, be compared not unfavorably with many modern industrial workers. Many men today are virtually condemned to celibacy by the difficulty of making a living. Slaves were often encouraged to marry by their masters, and once married, they were, in one important respect at least, in a far happier position than many of our modern workers. Things are made as difficult as possible for, say, a bank clerk or a civil servant who wishes to raise a family, but normal parenthood was one of the natural rights that the slave was free to exercise. The free man of today gives the best years of his life to the service of the firm from which he can be dismissed without redress if he is considered to be too old for his work. Modern industry gives to the employer virtually dictatorial powers. Labor is fluid, and a long-standing firm that has been amalgamated or merged may lose its identity, and a loss may be transformed into a profit by wholesale dismissals. A slave in a Christian household at least had security of tenure. He was always sure of food, clothes, and a roof over his head. When he could no longer work, he had to be kept.

I am prepared to concede that there were, of course, many bad slave owners, and it was indeed the difficulty of enforcing the Church's conception of slavery that rendered irresistible the demand for complete emancipation. But it is impossible to prove that slavery, which admittedly proved in practice to be incompatible with Christianity, was theoretically irreconcilable with the Christian view of life. It is, of course, useless to argue with people who, as the result of defective imagination, read back all their own prejudices into the remote past. There are people who are piously shocked because the primitive Church accepted as a matter of course an institution that was as integral a part of the ancient world as the trade unions are of modern

England, an institution that Christ has never condemned. Remember that our hypothetical emancipator could cite no text of Scripture and no saying of Christ in support of his views; and remember also that the sudden liberation of slaves throughout the Roman Empire would have produced an economic crisis from the catastrophic results of which the slaves would have been the first to suffer.

The modern Christian wholeheartedly condemns slavery not because the academic defense of Christian slavery, as I have called it, is easy to refute, but because the practical experience of centuries has proved that it is impossible to maintain those safeguards that alone render slavery reconcilable with Christianity.

We shall see that it was the evils of the African slave trade that transformed the attitude of the Church from one of dubious acquiescence into uncompromising hostility.

On the question of slavery, revelation, as we have seen, was silent, and Christians were accordingly left to discover for themselves by the slow process of trial and error that slavery could not be tolerated in a Christian state. Slavery did not disappear for many centuries, but the slavery that survived was radically different from the slavery of the pagan world. Slavery, indeed, was dramatically transformed by its first contact with Christianity.

Slaves were among the first members of the primitive Christian Church, for the apostles realized at the outset that the equality of all Christians before Christ was the inevitable conclusion from the Christian premise. "For as many of you as have been baptized into Christ have put on Christ. There is neither Jew nor Greek, there is neither bond nor free, there is neither male nor female: for ye are all one in Christ Jesus" (Gal. 3:27–28).

St. Paul drew no political conclusions from the premise of Christian equality, for he accepted the social structure as he found it. Broadly speaking, it is true that the divinitarian, as we may call the reformer who is inspired by the love of God, begins with the individual and hopes to affect the social structure through the individual, whereas the humanitarian begins with the social structure and hopes to improve the lot of the individual after he has improved his social environment.

From the first, St. Paul insisted that Christianity imposes obligations not only on slaves but on masters. The slave was to render willing service to his master, service inspired not by servile fear but by the love of God. "In singleness of your heart ... not with eyeservice, as men pleasers; but as the servants of Christ, doing the will of God from the heart; with good will doing service, as to the Lord, and not to men" (Eph. 6:5–7).

On his side the master was to forbear threatening and to remember that his master in Heaven was no respecter of persons. Above all, he was to "give unto your servants that which is just and equal" (Col. 4:1).

That all men are equal in the sight of God is a truism that the Christian of today takes for granted, and it is consequently difficult for us to realize that the granting of religious equality to slaves was, in effect, a silent revolution. Roman slaves had their own cults and religious reunions, but the religious equality of master and slave was a Christian innovation. Consequently, a Roman slave master could not prove the sincerity of his conversion to Christianity more effectively than by receiving the same sacrament as his slave, kneeling at the same altar. Christianity alone could reconcile the slave master to an innovation against which all his instincts must have revolted. Emancipated slaves were often raised to the priesthood, and, on two occasions, to the very Chair of St. Peter (Pius in the second century and Callistus in the third century).

Critics who profess to be shocked by the failure of the primitive Church to inaugurate a revolutionary campaign for the emancipation of slaves should at least give the Church credit for revolutionizing the status of the slave. In chapter 16, I have described the attitude to slavery of the most enlightened Stoics in the Roman world. Individual slaves might rise to positions of responsibility and dignity. Cicero's confidential secretary, Ino, is a case in point. But such promotion depended on the personality of the individual slave. The status of the slave *qua* slave has improved in exact proportion to the advance of Christianity.

I shall not attempt in this chapter even a bare summary of the very long process whereby the institution of slavery was slowly eroded by the Christian atmosphere. The process was admittedly slow, but it was nonetheless irresistible. There was no turning back. Each new advance on the road to liberty was firmly consolidated. Law and custom were constantly being revised in favor of the slave. The inalienable rights of the slave to marriage and the family were safeguarded from the first by the precepts of the Church and were later secured by legal enactment in the Theodosian Code. The slave, a mere chattel under Roman law, was promoted to the status of a man whom the law must protect. The violation of slave women, a recognized amusement among the Romans, was made punishable by death. The killing of a slave was no longer an incident that called neither for comment nor for criticism but was punishable as criminal homicide.

And side by side with these reforms of the rights of the slave, we find an ever-increasing pressure in favor of emancipation. Individual owners are encouraged either during their lives or on their deathbeds to free their slaves. Slavery is suppressed as a legal penalty. "We do not transfer," said the imperial lawgiver, "persons from a free condition into a servile — we who have so much at heart to raise slaves to liberty." The marriage of a master with a bondswoman emancipated all the children. The purpose of the code, indeed, was declared to be a hastening of the day when the republic would be inhabited by free men rather than by liberated slaves. Consequently, all presumptions in the Theodosian Code were deemed to be "in favor of liberty." If a will could be construed, by however forced an interpretation, as showing a desire to emancipate the slaves, the burden of proof rested on the heir if he intended to dispute the emancipation.

It is true that the first explicit attack on slavery does not occur before the ninth century. "Thou shalt possess no slave," writes St. Theodore of Studium, "neither for domestic service nor for the work of the fields; for man is made in the image of God." But the influence of Christianity was gradually transforming the slave into the serf. The relation of a serf to his lord was as of a clansman to his chief rather than as of a slave to his master. Serfdom was a vast improvement, for the serf was left in the full enjoyment of all personal rights, including complete freedom to dispose of his property, if any, and his freedom was restricted only insofar as he could not, without his lord's permission, leave the ground that it was his duty to cultivate. And just as slavery merged gradually into serfdom, so, in time, serfdom gradually disappeared from Christian lands. Meanwhile pronouncements of theologians reveal a growing realization of the fact that slavery should be abolished rather than reformed.

It is difficult for the modern reader to realize the sort of effect that must have been produced by the declaration of Pius II in 1462 that slavery was a great crime, or still more by Paul III's tremendous condemnation of the enslavement of the American Indians. Mr. D. B. Wyndham Lewis, in his excellent book *The Emperor of the West*, has summed up the effect of this Bull by an entertaining analogy. "If it were possible," he writes, to imagine a declaration issued officially by a modern Archbishop of Canterbury to the effect that Old Etonians are in the eyes of Almighty God the equals of Englishmen from the lesser public schools, the effect on modern England would much resemble the effect of Paul III's Bull on sixteenth-century Europe; for from the Bull Europe learned that those strange chocolate-skinned figures, with their high cheekbones and queer slanting eyes, were rational beings, capable of receiving all the Sacraments and having equal human rights before God with any Hidalgo of Spain or Lord Mayor of London, and that the penalty for exploiting them was excommunication.

The Bull minced no words. Exploiters of the Indians are "instruments of Satan," and by Apostolic authority all attempts made by them at enslaving the native are condemned and their commerce in slaves declared null and void. The Indians have the right fully and freely to possess and enjoy their liberty and disposal of themselves, and this must not be tampered with; for the forced servitude of human beings of any race, Christian or not, is a thing abhorrent and damnable.

It is true that this protest of Paul III was not as completely successful as he wished, but it is only the ill-informed who believe that the Church has always been in a position to impose its will when its will conflicted with popular opinion.

The faithful accepted without question the supreme authority of the Church in doctrine, for the profession of orthodoxy costs nothing in an orthodox state. But attempts to enforce the consequences of inconvenient doctrines were frequently met by effective passive resistance. The Church never ceased to denounce the duel, but the duel persists to this day in Catholic countries. And yet most duelists would have applauded the burning of the heretic who refused to accept the Church's view that dueling was wrong. Of course dueling is a sin, but there are times, so the duelist would argue, when a man of honor must be prepared to risk not only death but Hell.

The Church could always count on the support of Catholics, however slack, in its struggle with heresy, because even the least instructed Catholic realizes the mortal danger of heresy and because even those who were least disposed to put Catholicism into practice retained a great reverence for Catholicism in theory. But, though the faithful were all in favor of the extermination of heresy, the Church had to employ every diplomatic artifice to secure the least concession on points where Catholicism was in conflict with social customs or with the selfish interests of avaricious men. Sometimes the Church failed completely, as in the case of the duel; sometimes the Church was completely successful, as in the abolition of trial by ordeal; sometimes the Church was partially successful, as, for instance, in its attempt to suppress the plague of the Dark Ages, private war between feudal chiefs. The methods in this case are, indeed, an admirable example of that diplomacy that we must employ in dealing with intractable human nature. It would have been useless to threaten feudal chiefs with excommunication. It would, humanly speaking, have been as impossible to abolish private war at one stroke as to emancipate every slave in the early centuries of the Church. Consequently the Church began by coaxing the feudal chiefs into the acceptance of a weekend truce. Gradually this truce was extended to Thursdays and Fridays, and finally private war disappeared altogether.

Our secular humanitarians, who owe all that is noble in their humanitarianism to the Christianity that they repudiate, forget that the most important fact about slavery is not that emancipation was delayed but that emancipation was achieved. It is indeed the Christ whom they repudiate who provides the anti-Christian with his most effective argument. It is strange that the atheist never realizes that he gives away his own case when he taunts Christians with the contrast between the example of Christ and the evil deeds of those who profess and call themselves Christians. The wickedness of Christian slave traders is no argument for the atheist, for it is Christ and not the atheist who has opened our eyes to the evils of the slave trade. The worst evils of slavery would pass without comment in a world in which atheism reigned unchallenged. Indeed, the opponents of slavery may search the philosophy of atheism in vain for a single valid argument in support of liberty. The atheist is necessarily a determinist and is thereby stopped from protesting against slavery in the name of the liberty in which he does not believe. For if every man is, as the determinists believe, the slave of circumstances, why should one particular form of slavery to which we are all subjected excite so much moral indignation?

Again, if atheism be true, all the achievements of man are doomed to ultimate extinction in the final shipwreck of the solar system, and nothing of any permanent value is achieved on the surface of this planet. All souls, in consequence, are equally insignificant and equally valueless. It was not the doctrine of human worthlessness but the belief in the infinite value of every human soul that struck the fetters from the slave. It was in Christian lands that the slaves were first freed. It is mainly in the lands furthest removed from Christian influence that slavery still persists. It was in the apostate country that had repudiated Christianity and officially adopted atheism that slavery reappeared disguised as forced labor.

A Saint in the Slave Trade

The very gradualness of the process whereby slavery disappeared is indeed a striking example of the slow but irresistible effect of the Christian leaven. "No laws," writes Mr. Chesterton in *A Short History of England*,

> had been passed against slavery, and no dogmas had ever condemned it by definition, no new race or ruling caste had repudiated it, but it was gone. This silent and startling transformation is, perhaps, the best measure of the pressure of popular light in the Middle Ages, of how fast it was making new things in its spiritual factory. Like everything else in the medieval revolution, from its cathedrals to its ballads, it was anonymous as it was enormous. It is admitted everywhere that the conscious and active emancipators were the parish priests and the religious brotherhoods; but no name among them has survived, and no man among them has reached his reward in this world. Countless Clarksons and innumerable Wilberforces without political machinery or public fame worked at deathbeds and confessionals in all the villages of Europe; and the vast system of slavery vanished.... The Catholic type of Christianity was not merely an element, it was a climate; and in that climate a slave would not grow.

I did my best, in a book that I wrote many years ago, to pick holes in this passage, but without real success. I agree that some of the statements that Mr. Chesterton tells us are "admitted everywhere" would be disputed by the sort of people whose hatred of the Church deprives them of all power of sympathetic understanding of their own historical background, but I believe that the main argument of this passage would be conceded by the overwhelming majority of historians.

6

Theory and Practice

The Church, we have seen, was prepared to tolerate slavery under very definite restrictions. It was, as we shall learn, the failure of slave owners and slave traders to respect those rights that the Church demanded for the slave, which transformed the attitude of the Church from unenthusiastic acquiescence into determined opposition.

The contrast between slavery in Christian theory and slavery in Christian practice is perhaps no greater than the contrast between the teaching of Christ and the behavior of too many of His followers. I have never been able to discover why this admitted contrast, which was indeed the theme of so many of the more sorrowful sayings of Our Lord, should be exploited as an argument against the truth of Christianity or against the claims of Christ. Indeed, if Christians always behaved as Christians should behave, they would have proved Christ to be a false prophet, for Christ never prophesied that the waters of Baptism would eradicate every impulse inconsistent with the precepts of Christianity.

Christ foretold exactly what has happened. The leaven of Christianity works slowly, and the very gradualness of its triumph over human sin and human selfishness is precisely what Christ taught us to expect.

A Saint in the Slave Trade

Before the Renaissance, the overwhelming majority of Europeans accepted Christianity as readily and as unthinkingly as the majority of modern Europeans accept the evolutionary philosophy. Then, as now, only a small minority of professing Christians made a determined and partially successful effort to model their lives on Christ.

In Christian lands, positions of authority in the State will normally be held by men who profess Christianity, partly because Christianity is the religion of their country, and partly because, insofar as they believe anything, they are inclined to believe in Christianity. They are not necessarily insincere, but they remain uninfluenced in practice by the Faith of the creed that they profess and because their actions are determined not by the spirit of Christianity but by the governing motives of avarice, pride, and lust. While nominally acquiescing in the judgments of the Church, they will exercise all their ingenuity to discover an interpretation of those laws sufficiently elastic to justify any action that suits their pocket or gratifies their pride. In my last chapter, I set forth the four titles to slavery that the Church was prepared to recognize — among others, the right of just war and the condemnation for crime. The enslavement of the Indians provides a perfect illustration of the technique by which unprincipled men can travesty the spirit while endeavoring to preserve the forms of canon law. Here, for instance, is the substance of a proclamation issued by Alonso de Ojeda, servant of the very high and powerful kings of Castile and Leon, to the Indian population whom he desired to enslave.

First, the proclamation tells them of the creation of man.

Then it declares how God gave charge of all these nations to one man called St. Peter, that he should be the head of the human race, and have rule over them all, and fix his seat at Rome "as the fittest place for governing the world." ...

Having now established the papal power, the proclamation proceeds to inform the Indians, how a certain pope gave to the Catholic sovereigns all these western islands and this western continent, as appears from certain writings which the Indians are told they may see if they like (*que podeis ver si quisieredes*). Then they are told how well other islands who have had this notice have received His Majesty and obeyed him, listening without any resistance or delay to religious men, and becoming Christians, and how kind His Majesty has been to them. "Wherefore I entreat and require you," says Ojeda, "that after taking due time to consider this, you acknowledge the 'church' as sovereign lady of the world and the Pope in her name, and His Majesty, in his place as Lord of these isles and continent, and receive these religious men. If you do, His Majesty will greet you with all love and affection. But if you do not, I will enter with power into your land and will subdue you, and will take your wives and children and make slaves of them and do you all the mischief I can, as to Vassals that do not obey and will not receive their Lord. And I protest that all death and destruction which may come from this is your fault, and not His Majesty's or mine, or that of my men."[8]

This grotesque document, as Arthur Helps points out, was common form and was used not only by Ojeda but by all such

---

[8] Sir Arthur Helps, *The Spanish Conquest in America: And Its Relation to the History of Slavery and to the Government of Colonies*, vol. 2 (New York: Harper and Brothers, 1856), 235–236.

similar privateers. The wretched Indians who listened to it had only the haziest conception of the meaning of such words as *church*, even if the interpreters had done their duty. But as it was not in the interest of the privateers that the document should be understood, it is not uncharitable to suppose that the interpreters carried out their duties in a very perfunctory fashion. Whenever this proclamation had the desired effect, that is, whenever this proclamation had no effect at all, hostilities were immediately commenced and prisoners of war were branded and made slaves.

The hypocrisy whereby the Church's teaching on the four titles to lawful slavery was exploited to justify the most unblushing piracy had a great effect on the theologians, an effect that was reinforced by the appalling evils of the slave trade. The Church, as we have seen, was prepared to tolerate the theory that the slave owner had dominion over the time and labor of the slave; from which it logically followed that he had a right to transfer this dominion, by sale or otherwise, to another slave owner. In other words, if slavery could be reconciled with Christianity, slave trading, theoretically at least, could also be reconciled, provided—and provided only—that the inalienable rights of the slaves were not compromised in the transference by sale to another master. The Church, for instance, regarded such sales as sinful if a slave was sold apart from his wife or his children.

But though the Church was prepared theoretically to condone the slave trade, the attitude of theologians was transformed from grudging acquiescence to active opposition by the accumulation of facts that proved that the manner in which the African slave trade was carried out was anti-Christian in spirit and in practice. In 1462 the pope, Pius II, condemned the slave traffic.

The importation of African slaves into Spanish America began in 1500. The Spanish colonists clamored for non-European labor, since Europeans soon succumbed to the rigors of manual work in tropical climates. The slave trade was still further encouraged by the system of *asientos*, that is to say, monopolies or contracts sold by Spain to nations or individuals. The contractor bought the sole rights for importing a given number of African slaves for a given number of years. It needs no very lively stretch of imagination to realize that a contractor who had the right to import, say, one thousand slaves, would not lose much sleep satisfying himself that each of these slaves had lost his liberty in accordance with the four titles to slavery recognized by the Church.

The first contract was sold to the Genoese in 1517, and in 1713, as a result of the Peace of Utrecht, an *asiento* was granted to our country, the first of many, and throughout the eighteenth century our country enjoyed the distinction of taking the lead in this degraded form of commerce.

Fr. Claver's predecessor, Alfonso de Sandoval, and the Dominican Fr. Thomas Mercado have left us a well-documented picture of the slave trade as carried on in their day—that is, at the end of the sixteenth and the beginning of the seventeenth century. They wrote with the reserve of theologians who refused to be swayed by emotional reactions and who realized that a principle is not necessarily invalidated by evils that are not the inevitable consequence of the principle in question. They did not dispute the unanimous consensus of theologians of their day. They accepted the institution of slavery in theory as potentially reconcilable with Christian principles. They had no difficulty in proving that "the four titles to lawful slavery" were most grossly abused in practice. Sandoval, for instance, proved that "the right of just war" was a mere cover for inciting wars that were neither just nor necessary. There is abundant evidence to show that the African chieftains made war on each other simply and solely with a view to selling their prisoners of war to the African traders.

The second title to lawful slavery, "condemnation for crime," was even more flagrantly abused. Native kings were only too pleased to borrow a hint from Europe and to impose slavery as a punishment. Indeed, the chieftains balanced their budgets by inventing new offenses and by exporting to the Portuguese the "criminals" who had been condemned for imaginary crimes. Finally, when all else failed, the Portuguese cheerfully threw the "four titles to lawful slavery" overboard and indulged in piracy unashamed. Black agents called *Pumberos* invaded Africa provided with European goods, which they exchanged against slaves, and when exchange failed, they resorted to simple pillage.

It is consoling to reflect that conscience was stirring among the rulers of Europe. Fr. Mercado, the Dominican, describes the ever-increasing severity of the legislation with which the Christian kings sought to suppress the piracy of the Portuguese and to restrain the slave trade within the four walls of the much-abused four principles.

"Theologians," writes Miss Petre,

> were likewise busy with the question, for some anxious-minded persons wrote from Spain to Lisbon, saying that the theologians of Seville held grave doubts regarding the lawfulness of the traffic, and asking what was the opinion of Portuguese authorities. They were answered briefly that there were not two systems of justice and theology, and that what was taught in one place was taught in another, with the difference that the Portuguese theologians were even more severe in the judgment of a practice with which they were most nearly concerned.

Father Mercado sums up by the two following conclusions: (1) The purchase and sale of Negroes in Cabo Verde
is, in itself, lawful and just. (2) That, granting the tales
we hear, and likewise the truth and reality of them, it is a
mortal sin to exercise this trade, and the merchants who
traffic in bringing Negroes to Cabo Verde live in a bad
and dangerous state.

It is well that we should remember such facts, for we
are too apt to think that those questions were only opened
in our own century.[9]

In other words, Fr. Mercado was prepared to admit that the
purchase and sale of slaves is theoretically consistent with Christianity, but he was driven by practical experience of the slave
trade heartily to denounce a traffic perhaps even more tragic in
its consequences to the slave trader than to the slave.

---

[9] Maude Petre, *Aethiopum Servus*, 128–129.

7

The Vilest Ever

Go on, in the Name of God, and in the power
of His might, until even American slavery (the vilest
that ever saw the sun) shall vanish before it.

—Wesley's last letter to Wilberforce

We shall never understand the problem that confronted Claver unless we have formed a picture of the circumstances in which the African was normally enslaved in his own continent and the conditions under which he was transported to the New World. The condition of the slave once he had landed may not have merited this famous phrase, "the vilest that ever saw the sun," but the conditions endured during the voyage involved a degree of physical suffering at least as great as that which human beings have ever been called upon to endure for a prolonged period of time.

It is unnecessary to darken the shadows of our picture by an imaginary contrast between the alleged Arcadian simplicity in which the simple African lived and the miseries of his subsequent fate. Such pictures, though common in the tracts of abolitionists, bear no relation to reality.

Africa has an ancient tradition of slavery. In the centuries preceding the discovery of America, Mohammedan conquerors and traders had penetrated into the remotest districts. They had perfected the technique of playing off one petty chieftain against another by inciting them to wars, and the prisoners who were the result of these wars were purchased from the victors and sold as slaves in other parts of the continent. The African chiefs, indeed, often preferred to enrich themselves by such means rather than by industry and agriculture.

There was, again, an unceasing demand for slaves to supply the needs of Mohammedan rulers on the Mediterranean littoral. The hardships of slaves who were marched in chained gangs across the desert need not be described. They are being endured even at the present day in Abyssinia. There is, however, one respect in which slavery in Mohammedan countries differed from black slavery in America. The Mohammedan slave has never been regarded as a creature of a different genus from his master. They were not despised as subhuman by their Arab owners. Indeed, in the varying fortunes of war a slave might become a petty king and perhaps be enslaved again. The Mohammedan trader was certainly no less brutal and callous than the white trader, but the slave, when he reached his final destination, was not without hope that his master might treat him as a fellow human being, whose status was accidental. Among the Mohammedans, the slave often rose high in the confidence of his master, because he succeeded in amusing his master by his conversation.

The internal African slave trade inflicted the maximum degree of active hardship, the American slave trade the maximum of passive hardship. Active hardship may have certain redeeming qualifications. Rest follows fatigue, food hunger, and drink thirst. The horrors of the sea voyage were mainly passive. Suffering without dignity, misery without relief.

The slave trade between Africa and America ceased before the introduction of steam navigation and, in the age of sail conditions, varied very little. The slaves with whom Claver came into contact had passed through experiences similar to or even identical with those described by Wilberforce in the following passage:

Many of the sufferings of these wretched beings are of a sort for which no legislative regulations can provide a remedy. Several of them, indeed, arise necessarily out of their peculiar circumstances, as connected with their condition on shipboard. It is necessary to the safety of the vessel to secure the men by chains and fetters. It is necessary to confine them below during the night, and in very stormy weather during the day also. Often it happens, with the numbers allowed to be taken, especially when some of those epidemic diseases prevail, and when men of different countries and languages, or of opposite tempers, are linked together, that such scenes take place as are too nauseous for description. Still in rough weather their limbs must be excoriated by lying on the boards; still they will often be wounded by fetters; still food and exercise will be deemed necessary to present the animal in good condition at the place of sale; still some of them will loathe their food, and be averse to exercise, from the joint effect perhaps of sea-sickness and mental uneasiness; and still, while in this state, there will probably be sulkiness; and eating and dancing in their fetters will be enforced by stripes; still the high netting will be necessary, that standing precaution of an African ship against acts of suicide; but more than all, still must the diseases of

the mind remain entire, nay, they may perhaps increase
in force, from the attention being less called off by the
urgency of bodily suffering; the anguish of husbands torn
from their wives, wives from their husbands, and parents
from their children; the pangs arising from the consideration that they are separated for ever from their country,
their friends, their relations, remain the same.[10]

A more detailed account is contained in the evidence given
by Falconbridge, a ship's surgeon, before a committee of inquiry.
He describes the manner in which the human cargo was stowed:

The men Negroes, on being brought aboard ship, are immediately fastened together two by two, by handcuffs on
their wrists, and by irons riveted on their legs.... They are
frequently stowed so close as to admit of no other posture
than lying on their sides. Neither will the height between
decks, unless directly under the grating, permit them the
indulgence of an erect posture, especially where there are
platforms, which is generally the case. These platforms
are a kind of shelf, about eight or nine feet in breadth,
extending from the side of the ship towards the centre.
They are placed nearly midway between the decks, at the
distance of two or three feet from each deck. Upon these
the Negroes are stowed in the same manner as they are
on the deck underneath.... It often happens that those
who are placed at a distance from the buckets, in endeav-
ouring to get to them, tumble over their companions, in

[10]   William Wilberforce, *A Letter on the Abolition of the Slave Trade;
       Andressed and Other Inhabitants of Yorkshire* (London: Luke Han-
       sard and Sons, 1807), 99–101.

consequence of their being shackled. These accidents, although unavoidable, are productive of continual quarrels, in which some of them are always bruised. In this distressed situation they desist from the attempt.... This results in a fresh source of broils and disturbances, and tends to render the situation of the poor captive wretches still more uncomfortable.

In favourable weather they are fed upon deck, but in bad weather the food is given to them below. Numberless quarrels take place among them during their meals, more especially when they are put upon short allowance, which frequently happens. In that case the weak are obliged to be content with a very scanty portion. Their allowance of water is about half a pint each, at every meal.

Upon the Negroes refusing to take sustenance, I have seen coals of fire, glowing hot, put on a shovel, and placed so near their lips as to scorch and burn them, and this has been accompanied with threats of forcing them to swallow the coals, if they any longer persisted in refusing to eat. These means have generally the desired effect. I have also been credibly informed that a certain captain in the slave trade poured melted lead on such of the Negroes as obstinately refused their food....

The Negroes are far more violently affected by seasickness than Europeans. It frequently terminates in death, especially among the women. The exclusion of the fresh air is among the most intolerable of their sufferings. Most ships have air-ports; but, whenever the sea is rough and the rain heavy, it becomes necessary to shut these and every other conveyance by which air is admitted. The fresh air being thus excluded, the Negroes' rooms very soon grow intolerably hot. The confined air, rendered noxious by the effluvia exhaled from their bodies, and by being repeatedly breathed, soon produces fevers and fluxes, which generally carry off great numbers of them.... My profession requiring it, I frequently went down among them, till at length their apartment became so extremely hot as to be only sufferable for a very short time. But the excessive heat was not the only thing that rendered their situation intolerable. The deck, that is, the floor of their rooms, was so covered with the blood and mucus which had proceeded from them in consequence of the flux, that it resembled a slaughter-house.... Numbers of the slaves having fainted, they were carried on deck, where several of them died; and the rest were with great difficulty restored.... By only continuing among them for about a quarter of an hour, I was so overcome by the heat, stench, and foul air, that I had nearly fainted; and it was not without assistance that I could get upon deck.[11]

The above passage describes the conditions in a slaver which sailed with a complement a hundred short of her capacity, there being regulations that laid down the number of slaves that might be carried in proportion to the tonnage. Falconbridge then describes conditions in a vessel that carried more than three slaves to each ton:

The slaves were so crowded that they were obliged to lie one upon another. This occasioned such a mortality

[11] Alexander Falconbridge, *An Account of the Slave Trade on the Coast of Africa* (London: J. Phillips, 1788), 19–25.

among them, that, without meeting with unusual bad weather, or having a longer voyage than common, nearly one half of them died before the ship arrived in the West Indies.... The place allotted for the sick Negroes is under the half-deck, where they lie on the bare plank. Thus, those who are emaciated frequently have their skin, and even their flesh, entirely rubbed off, by the motion of the ship, from the prominent parts of the shoulders, elbows, and hips, so as to render the bones in those parts quite bare. The excruciating pain ... frequently for several weeks.... The surgeon, upon going between decks in the morning, frequently finds several of the slaves dead, and sometimes a dead and a living Negro fastened by their irons together.[12]

It would be difficult to believe that conditions of such abject misery could be aggravated by any conceivable cause, but it would seem that this was not the case, and that the slaves had sufficient vitality left to deepen their distress by internecine feuds. The races of Africa are no less diverse than those of Europe, and as many as forty different languages were sometimes spoken on one slave ship. The petty king of a dominant fighting race might find himself chained to the caitiff of a servile tribe. Suicide was frequent whenever the opportunity presented itself. On one occasion when certain slaves had broken loose and thrown themselves into the sea, those who had been captured before they succeeded in following their example were shot and hanged, an illogical deterrent for their fellows from attempting to imitate them.

---

[12] Ibid., 26, 27–28.

A Saint in the Slave Trade

Captain Wauchope, R.N., reporting on the capture of a Portuguese slaver, wrote:

> After capture, I went on board, and such a scene of horror it is not easy to describe. The long-boat on the booms, and the deck aft, were crowded with little children, sickly, poor little unhappy things, some of them rather pretty, and some much marked and tattooed: much pains must have been taken by their miserable parents to ornament them.
>
> The women lay between decks, aft, much crowded and perfectly naked; they were not barred down, the hatchway, a small one, being off; but the place for the men was too horrible: the wretches, chained two and two, gasping and striving to get at the bars of the hatchways, and such a steam and stench as to make it intolerable even to look down. It requires much caution at first, in allowing them to go on deck, as it is a common practice for them to jump overboard to get quit of their misery.[13]

Many students of the slave trade have been perplexed by the lack of consideration for their own interests shown by the traders. The deterioration of their stock might have been reduced by a little more consideration for their human cargo. But we must remember that the slave trade involves great hardship on all concerned. The voyage itself, in brigs of four hundred tons, was often dangerous.

Moreover, a moral taint always attaches itself to the slave trade, and only men of blunt sensibilities would engage in it.

---

[13] Sir Thomas Foxwell Buxton, *The African Slave Trade and Its Remedy* (London: John Murray, 1840), 157.

Once involved in this troubled business, they were forced to do constant violence to their moral nature, with the result that they often developed an active malevolence against the slaves, upon whom they vented all their dull resentment against the fate that had enticed them into so degraded a profession.

They claimed that they were regarded with contempt by decent society, that is, by society that was decent enough to despise the slave trader while availing itself of his services. They seem to have derived a sullen pleasure from humiliating the slaves entrusted to their care as if to emphasize the vast gulf that separated the lowest of the white race from the best specimens of the black.

8

The Forerunners of Emancipation

The Church finds work for all men of goodwill, for the divinitarian mainly interested in the individual and for the social reformer mainly interested in ideas.

Three men, all concerned directly or indirectly with the slave trade, may be taken as types of three different classes of Christian reformers. The first is Wilberforce, who devoted his life to campaigning on behalf of the slaves but who never came into personal contact with slaves and consequently was never in a position to relieve the distress or save the soul of the individual slave. Secondly, there is Fr. Claver, whose life is the theme of the first part of this book. The Catholic Church produces many saints like Fr. Claver, who have a vocation for the reform of individuals rather than of institutions, saints whose first instinct is to relieve immediate distress and bind up the wounds of those in their immediate neighborhood, while leaving to others the task of changing the institution responsible for the evil that they deplore.

Fr. Claver was so occupied with slaves that he had little time to think about slavery. He was a simple man, and so far from regretting the slave trade, he would probably have rejoiced in it as an instrument for the salvation of souls. He knew that the

A Saint in the Slave Trade

Africans lived in their own countries in conditions of spiritual degradation, and he believed that the slave traders had rendered them a real service by bringing them within the reach of Christian Baptism. This simpleminded saint held with passionate conviction the belief that it was better to die a Christian slave at Cartagena than a native chieftain in the Congo. The slave trade was full of perils for the slave trader, but, on the balance, a boon to the slave. Grotesque though this conclusion must seem, the intelligent humanist must concede that it is a logical conclusion from the Catholic premise, which is one of many reasons why the intelligent humanist rejects with such scorn a premise that he never condescends to examine. And yet Claver, though not a conscious reformer of slavery, was unconsciously preparing the way for emancipation. Two hundred years were to pass before the slaves were free, but the campaign for emancipation owed more than it ever guessed to the labors of men like Fr. Claver, who raised these wretched slaves not only in their own estimation but in the estimation of their Christian fellows. It was difficult to relegate to the category of mere brutes the slaves whom the saint had kissed.

Finally, there are Catholics who combine both attitudes. Fr. Alfonso de Sandoval, Claver's predecessor in Cartagena, combined Claver's love for the individual victims of slavery with Wilberforce's passionate enthusiasm for social reform.

Sandoval belonged to a distinguished family. His father had first come to Lima on an official mission of some importance. The boy's education had been entrusted to the Jesuits, and in due course, Sandoval entered the order and dedicated his life to the apostolate of the slaves. As soon as a slave vessel reached the harbor, he hurried along with his interpreter. His first care was to baptize the dying and to prepare them for a Christian death.

It is less surprising that this attendance on the dying should be part of the regular routine on the arrival of a ship than that there were any slaves left alive to baptize. These unfortunates made the voyage packed in bundles of six, their necks chained and their feet shackled to their neighbors'. The normal passage lasted two months, and the normal loss in transit was about a third of the living cargo. On one occasion, no fewer than 120 out of a cargo of 500 died in one night alone.

The shattered wrecks struggled off the ship onto dry land, bleeding, ulcerous, and diseased, and were herded into a yard. "One huge mass of putrid life and suffering." It called for a high degree of heroism even to approach the stench and squalor of such surroundings. Even Sandoval himself, "when he received notice of the arrival of a Negro vessel, was covered instantly with a cold and death-like sweat at the recollection of what he had endured on the last occasion; nor did the experience and practice of years ever accustom him to it."[14]

Of such heroic endurances Fr. Claver proved himself to be an ardent imitator, but whereas Claver was interested only in slaves, Sandoval was interested in slavery. He collected and collated facts about the slave trade from different quarters, not only from slaves but from slave traders who were troubled about their prospects in the next world and who consulted him not only in the confessional but outside the confessional about the state of their souls. He gathered together all relevant evidence with a careful patience that would have endeared him to Mrs. Sidney Webb and wrote a most valuable book that is, indeed, one of our principal sources of information about the slave trade.

[14] From *Aethiopum Servus*, by Maude Petre, a fascinating study of Peter Claver.

A Saint in the Slave Trade

In the course of this book Sandoval wholeheartedly con-demned the traffic in slaves. Nor was Sandoval, the Jesuit, unique as a campaigner against these evils. Sandoval tried to do for the African slaves what the Dominicans attempted to do for the Indians, and their campaign would undoubtedly meet with the wholehearted approval of our modern humanitarians. The story is worth telling.

Missionary work among the native Indians began with the discovery of the New World. Before St. Ignatius had organized missionary enterprise and the missionary activities of his order, Pope Leo X promulgated a Bull conferring on the Franciscan Order extensive rights for the evangelization of the new territory. Peter of Ghent, a lay brother of that order and a relative of the emperor Charles V, founded a school for Indian noblemen and their children, which, in the early sixteenth century, was visited by as many as a thousand pupils.

It was not long before the Dominicans began to play an active part in the conversion of the Indians. They identified themselves with their interests and championed them against the Spanish conquistadores who had virtually enslaved them. The great Do-minican Bartolomé de Las Casas devoted his life to the Indians and obtained from Charles V a remarkable charter of liberties. In the course of his life's work, which was devoted to securing a practical enforcement of the emperor's command, he crossed the ocean no fewer than twelve times.

It was, indeed, his devotion to his beloved Indians that was responsible for his tragic advocacy of the importation of African slaves, an advocacy that he was bitterly to regret, but which was inspired at the time by the hope that the Indians would be unmolested if only the supply of African slaves were sufficient to meet all demands—a policy that cannot be defended.

The early Spanish colonists of the New World were a tough crowd. An Indian king once asked a priest whether the door of Heaven was open to Spaniards. "Yes, to good Spaniards."

"Then let me go to Hell," said the Indian, "that I may not come where they are."

The colonists were convinced that Europe could not supply the labor that they desired, since non-Europeans alone would endure servile labor in that climate. They were faced with ruin by the liberation of the Indian slaves under the laws that were the result of Las Casas's campaign. It is surprising that Las Casas could carry on his work in face of the violent hatred that he provoked, but the Catholic Church has always possessed one great advantage over Protestant churches in such cases. The champion of the oppressed, particularly if he is a priest, wields a very real weapon that no Protestant minister can wield. The oppressors whom Las Casas attacked were violent and brutal, but they were Catholics. And much as they might hate Las Casas as a man, they respected his office and the powers that that office conferred. His refusal of absolution to those who continued to defy the regulations for the employment of Indians was, perhaps, one of the many deciding influences that led to the triumph of his cause.

Las Casas wins from our modern humanitarian the approval that they might not concede to Claver, for the eloquence with which he defended his Indians was outdone by the violence with which he attacked their oppressors. Whereas love was the dominant power in Claver's life, Las Casas flavored his affection for the Indians with a good dose of honest hatred for their oppressors.

Las Casas would not have succeeded had he not enjoyed throughout his campaign the support of those great sovereigns Ferdinand and Isabella of Spain.

A Saint in the Slave Trade

As the fame of Claver has eclipsed Sandoval, so the fame of Las Casas has dimmed the reputation of the Dominican Fathers who prepared the way for Las Casas and carried their championship of the Indians to the court of Spain and whose courage in defense of the weak was one of the main factors in Las Casas's conversion.

This movement may have been said to have begun with a little group of Dominican friars, fifteen in number, living under the government of their Vicar.[15] From silent disapproval these good friars passed rapidly to public protest.

They therefore decided that their views should be put before the inhabitants of San Domingo from the pulpit. They accordingly agreed on and signed the protest that they wished to make, and Brother Antonio Montecino was selected to deliver this sermon. He seems to have possessed one essential qualification, for he was, we are told, a man of "great asperity in reprehending vice."

The principal persons of San Domingo were warned by the friars that a sermon of unusual interest on a matter of great importance was to be delivered. Consequently, the church was packed when Fr. Antonio ascended the pulpit and chose for his text a portion of the Gospel for the day: "I heard the voice of one crying in the wilderness."

"We have only a short account of the sermon," writes Helps, but we may imagine that it was an energetic discourse: for indeed, when anybody has anything to say, he can generally say it worthily. And here, instead of nice points of doctrine (over which, and not unreasonably, men can become eloquent, ingenious, wrathful, intense), was an evil uplifting itself before the eyes of

---

[15] The story is told in a book that was published in 1848, *The Conquerors of the New World*, by Sir A. Helps (238ff.).

all men, and respecting which neither preacher nor hearers could entrench themselves behind generalities. He told them that the sterile desert was an image of the state of their consciences: and then he declared with "very piercing and terrible words" (*palabras muy pungitivas y terribles*) that "the voice" pronounced that they were living in "mortal sin" by reason of their tyranny over these innocent people, the Indians. What authority was there for the imposition of this servitude? What just ground for these wars? How could the colonists rightly insist upon such cruel labors as they did from the Indians, neglecting all care of them both in the things of Heaven and those of earth? Such Spaniards had no more chance of salvation than Moors or Turks.

I almost hear during the discourse, the occasional clang of arms as men turned angrily about to one another, and vowed that this must not go on any longer. They heard the discourse out, however, and went to dinner. After dinner, the principal persons conferred together for a short time, and then set off for the friary to make a fierce remonstrance. When they had come to the friary, which, from its poor construction, might rather have been called a shed than a friary, the Vicar, Peter de Cordova, received them and listened to their complaint. They insisted upon seeing the preacher, Father Antonio, declaring that he had preached "delirious things," and that he must make retraction next Sunday. A long parley took place, in the course of which Peter de Cordova told them that the sermon was not the words of one man, but of the whole Dominican community. The angry deputation exclaimed that if Father Antonio did not unsay what he had said, the friars had better get ready their goods to embark for

Spain. "Of a truth, my Lords," replied the vicar, "that will give us little trouble"; which was true enough, for (as Las Casas tells us) all that the friars possessed—their books, clothes, and vestments for the Mass might have gone into two trunks. At last the colonists went away, upon the understanding that the matter would be touched upon next Sunday, and, as the remonstrants supposed, an ample apology would be offered them.

The next Sunday came; there was no occasion this time to invite anybody to come to church, for all the congregation were anxious to come, rejoicing in being about to hear an apology to themselves from the pulpit. After Mass, Father Antonio was again seen walking to the pulpit, and he gave out the text from the thirty-sixth chapter of Job, the third verse: "Repetam scientiam meam a principio et operatorem meum probabo justum" (I will repeat my knowledge from the beginning and prove my Maker just). Those of his audience who understood Latin, and were persons of any acuteness, perceived immediately what would be the drift of this sermon—no whit less unsavoury to them than the last. And so it was. Father Antonio only repeated his former facts, clinched his former arguments, and insisted upon his former conclusion. Moreover, he added that the Dominicans would not confess any man who made incursions among the Indians, and this the colonists might publish, and write to whom they pleased at Castile. The congregation heard Father Antonio out; and this time they did not go to the friary; but they determined to send a complaint to the King, and afterwards to dispatch a Franciscan (friar against friar) to argue their case at Court. Thither the colonists had already sent two agents to plead for having the Indians assigned to them for two or three lives, or in perpetuity.[16]

The Franciscan who was chosen for this embassy was Alonso di Espinal. The Dominicans possessed full resources for a similar mission, as fortunately two or three pious persons provided the funds, and Fr. Antonio was in due course sent to Spain to counteract the propaganda of Fr. Alonso. But whereas all doors were open to the Franciscan, as he was pleading the cause of the powerful, Fr. Antonio was little befriended and found official doors closed to him and "porters very peremptory."

But no peremptory porters could defeat a man who combined the fire of the divinitarian with the aggressive energy of our modern reformers. He bided his time patiently, hung round the doorways of the palace, watched until the porter was busily engaged in conversation with somebody else, dived past him, and gate-crashed his way into the royal presence. He made such an impression upon the king that the king insisted on the appointment of a junta, a sort of Royal Commission, to which the Franciscans and the Dominicans were to have free access. But once again Fr. Antonio was defeated in his attempt to obtain a fair hearing. Finally, he resolved on a bold step — the conversion of his special adversary, the Franciscan. He accordingly waylaid him one day and thus commenced his address: "Have you anything," he said, "to take out of this life with you but that ragged robe, full of unmentionable insects, which you carry on your shoulders?" This, as Helps remarks, was not "a winning mode of

[16] Sir Arthur Helps and Michael Oppenheim, *The Spanish Conquest in America: And Its Relation to the History of Slavery and to the Government of Colonies*, vol. 1 (London: John Lane, 1900), 177–178.

address," but Fr. Antonio showed greater skill in the course of this conversation than this opening gambit promised. He informed the Franciscan that he was being used as a tool, that he was imperiling the reward of a life of sanctity in a cause that could not possibly benefit him; in other words, that he was doing the devil's work without being paid for it even in the devil's wages. The Franciscan was converted and thereafter gave Fr. Antonio full information as to what was happening in the junta, information of which Fr. Antonio made the best possible use.

And in due course, as we have seen, Las Casas carried to a successful conclusion the campaign that these brave Dominicans had launched. Indeed, it was the sermons of the Dominicans that first sowed in Las Casas's soul the seeds of conversion. He himself had been refused absolution by the Dominicans because he possessed Indian slaves, a refusal that he resented at the time, but which awakened in his own mind the first doubt as to the righteousness of his conduct.

We see, then, that before the Jesuits arrived in 1572, two great religious orders, Dominicans and Franciscans, were busying themselves with the temporal and spiritual welfare of the native Indians.

Catholic missions have in general been more successful in identifying themselves with the needs of the people among whom they worked than the missions of "national" churches, which have always had to struggle against the charge, often unjust, of being the advance guard of the political or commercial domination of the nation with which they are identified.

Robert Louis Stevenson, for instance, has contrasted the achievements of the Society of Jesus in California with the activities of the "greedy land-thieves and sacrilegious gunmen." "So ugly a thing," he continues, "may our Anglo-Saxon Protestantism appear beside the doings of the Society of Jesus."

In Peru and Bolivia, the Jesuits discovered more than a hundred Indian tribes. They instructed the natives in the art of hut building and taught them various industries; they founded schools and saved the perishing traditions of the Inca civilization from extinction. Often they decided the issues of peace and war. The archbishop of La Plata, for instance, reported to the king of Spain that "the Jesuits, with no help other than their own zeal, accomplished in a short space of time a task which it has been found impossible to carry out by means of large armies and the expenditure of vast sums of money. They turned enemies into friends and converted the wildest and most intractable of nations into Your Majesty's obedient subjects."

Indeed, the Jesuits were worthy rivals of the Dominicans in their championship of the natives against the white planter. In North America they were instrumental in suppressing the practice of holding slave hunts. One Jesuit, indeed, went so far as to write a play in the native dialect in which the Europeans were held up to ridicule and contempt, and their vices satirized. The cast was composed entirely of Indians, and Indians in the neighborhood were invited to witness this edifying performance.

This incident appears to have been unique, perhaps fortunately, for the social reformers of those days who were ready to carry their protests to the courts of kings showed few signs of anticipating the more modern technique of inciting the oppressed against their rulers. The reforms, for instance, for which Fr. Antonio campaigned, provided no easy road to power, to political office, or to prestige. He pleaded unencouraged by plaudits from the oppressed for whom he spoke, and he carried on an apparently hopeless campaign undeterred by the opposition of the rich and powerful. In those days, social reform was not yet a career.

9

Contrasts

Before I bring this part of my book to a close, I must answer the question that many of my readers may already have asked. The Church, as we have seen, was prepared to tolerate slavery under certain safeguards, clearly defined by the theologians. The slave must not be deprived of his natural rights, among which not the least important was the right to marry and the right to parenthood. I have insisted on the vast contrast between the status of the slave under Christianity and the status of the slave under paganism. "All of which," I can hear the indignant reader exclaim, "is just eyewash. On your own showing, nobody seems to have bothered much what the theologians said."

I disagree. Even the ludicrous efforts made by the slave pirates to wangle their villainies and to give them the appearance of legality show that these men dared not openly flout the ruling of the Church. I do not, of course, maintain that the laws of the Church were invariably obeyed in the letter and in the spirit. In this, as in every matter, practice fell short of Christian theory. Slave owners varied just as other people vary. At one end of the scale, you would find conscientious Christians who treated their slaves with every consideration, and at the other end of the scale, there would be brutes who treated their slaves as brutes.

A Saint in the Slave Trade

The contrast between the status of the slave in Catholic and in Protestant colonies is striking evidence of the debt that the slaves owed to the theologians of the Catholic Church. The slave in Catholic countries possessed what the slave in Protestant colonies did not possess: a powerful protector who was answerable not to a national and secular government but to an international Church. Fr. Claver, for instance, was a member of an order with branches in different countries and was the priest of a Church that claimed universal jurisdiction. Slave owners and slave traders might do their best to evade or misinterpret the laws of the Church, but they did not dare to deny their validity. The Catholic priest could appeal with complete confidence to the teaching of his Church, knowing well that no Catholic would dare to deny, under pain of heresy, the authoritative character of that teaching. The only possibility of argument with the Catholic slave owner would arise out of the application of the Church's teaching. A Protestant clergyman, on the other hand, in a Protestant colony, such as Jamaica, who evoked the authority of his church in an attempt to defend the rights of the slave, might have been reminded that his church took its theology from Parliament and that it was for Parliament and not for the episcopacy to decide the rights of the slave. In those days, few Anglicans would have been prepared to assert, as the founders of the Oxford movement were later to assert, the spiritual independence of the Church of England.

The right of the slave to marry was never denied in Catholic colonies, and consequently never needed to be reasserted, but it was not until 1826 that the Jamaican House of Assembly proposed for the first time in that Protestant colony that slaves should be granted the right of marriage and then only with their masters' consent—a reservation that, in effect, invalidated the law.

The Jamaican House of Assembly strongly resented the least suggestion that the clergy had any right of spiritual protection as far as the slaves were concerned. The Protestant clergy, unlike the Catholic priesthood, represented no supernational authority. A Protestant clergyman might lament the promiscuous immorality of the slaves among whom he worked and might desire to regularize these unions by marriage. But he was powerless to affect the widespread view that the slaves belonged to a subhuman species, and that nothing could be gained by insisting on the introduction of Christian marriage. Miss Petre quotes the words of a local doctor that every attempt to check these evils by introducing the marriage ceremony would be utterly impracticable and perhaps of dangerous consequence.

Now, Fr. Claver, as we know, made no protest against the institution of slavery or against the slave trade. He knew that the Church permitted slavery and the sale of slaves. But he also knew that the Church declared that slaves possessed certain very definite rights, and he invariably acted on the assumption that no slave owner could possibly be so foolish as to challenge those rights.

In Protestant Jamaica, no slave marriage could take place before the clergyman had obtained the consent of the slave owner, and this consent was normally refused. Fr. Claver never dreamt of asking any slave owner for permission to marry his slaves. He cheerfully married every slave who wished to be married, knowing full well that he would be supported by the Catholic laws of a Catholic country.

"A Negro in Cartagena," as Miss Petre says, "was, on the whole, credited with a human soul; our slave-owners of Jamaica talked lightly of their seraglios of 'black cattle,' and asked whether an orang-outang husband was not a worthy partner for a Hottentot woman. The accounts of this island remind us of slavery in pagan Rome." Miss Petre quotes a pamphlet written in 1788 by a Protestant who compares the colony disadvantageously with the Spanish settlements, and says: "If a general emancipation of the slaves should not be effected, ought we to be less liberal than the French and Spanish, who, having planted Christianity in their islands, are by no means so severe in their discipline, and yet have experienced no bad effect from either?"

It is to the glory of Protestantism that most of the great leaders in the cause of emancipation were Protestants, a fact to which Cardinal Manning draws attention in a famous passage. It is, however, only just to remember that the Protestant conscience was troubled by the memory of graver wrongs and that there was, in consequence, a greater need to emancipate the slaves in Protestant than in Catholic colonies.

"The crowning blow to Dickens's ideal conception of America," writes Mr. Kingsmill in his study of Dickens,

> was the slave-system, which before leaving England he may have hoped might be an anomaly which could be partially justified by its working. Against its actual working, and against the pretence that public opinion was a sufficient check on its abuses, he delivered in *American Notes* an attack which, being unwarped by personal resentments, is superior in force and sincerity to any of his more famous attacks on social abuses in England.
>
> "Public opinion!" he wrote. "Why, public opinion in the slave States *is* slavery, is it not?... Public opinion has made the laws, and denied the slaves legislative protection. Public opinion has knotted the lash, heated the branding iron, loaded the rifle, and shielded the murderer.

Public opinion threatens the abolitionist with death, if he venture to the South; and drags him with a rope about his middle, in broad unblushing noon, through the first city in the East." After some further examples of the mitigating effect of public opinion, Dickens concluded with a number of newspaper advertisements of runaway slaves, from which he said one could infer what pressure of public opinion there was on slave owners to treat their slaves humanely. Among the clues to identify runaways which he quoted were: "Has no toes on the left foot." "Has one ear cropped." "Has one jaw broken." "A few days before she went off, I burnt her with a hot iron, on the left side of her face. I tried to make the letter M." "His left eye out, some scars from a dirk on and under his left arm, and much scarred with the whip." "Has a considerable scar across his breast and each arm, made by a knife; loves to talk much of the goodness of God."[17]

The significance of these atrocities is not only that they occurred but that public opinion was so callous that the perpetrators of such atrocities dared to advertise these horrible facts in the public press.

[17] Hugh Kingsmill, *The Sentimental Journey: A Life of Charles Dickens.*

10

Claver in Cartagena

From the moment that the coast of Spain dropped below the Eastern waves, Spain passed out of Claver's thoughts forever. In the years that followed, he was never known to mention his native land or those whom he had left there.

He won all hearts on the long voyage to America by his restless devotion to the sick. He dined at the captain's table and bore up manfully under this distressing honor. The food at the captain's table was better than elsewhere, and Claver loved good food, provided he was not forced to eat it. His sanctity was always controlled by common sense, and the dainties that he removed from the captain's table proved a tactful introduction to the catechismal instruction of the sick. Man cannot live by bread alone. No, nor can he live by spiritual food alone, a fact of which Claver showed himself fully aware in all his relations with the slaves.

Claver left Spain unordained, for he could not believe himself to be worthy yet of the supreme dignity of the priesthood. On landing at Cartagena, he was sent to the college of Santa Fe for two years in order to complete his theological studies. The college, however, was so poverty-stricken and understaffed that theological lectures were postponed and Claver found himself occupying in turn the positions of sacristan, porter, and cook.

A Saint in the Slave Trade

He felt that this was all very suitable and asked his superior for permission to remain a lay brother for the rest of his life. Claver's humility must at times have been maddening. It was useless to argue with him, and the superior fell back on the first principles of the order and told Claver to be guided by obedience.

After completing the theological course, he sat for a rigorous examination. He was under the impression that this exacting test was a prelude to receiving Holy Orders and was unaware of the higher honors that were awaiting him. "Is so much theology," he exclaimed, "necessary in order to be able to receive ordination and baptize a few poor Negroes?" When he learned that he had been examined to discover whether he was fit to be admitted to the degree of professed Father, the most honorable degree of the Jesuit Order (the only degree that irrevocably binds the Jesuit to the order), he was overwhelmed with humiliation. "If I had known this," he exclaimed, "I would either not have answered at all, or I would have answered much worse than I did, for I am totally unworthy of this honor." Before taking his final vows, he spent yet a third year of novitiate in the newly established Jesuit house at Thonga. He was very happy among the novices at Thonga, and his kindly memories of this house persisted till his death. Indeed, as he lay dying, he sent to the House of Thonga, as the most precious pledge of his affection, the book that had been given him by his old friend the porter.

"I send it," he wrote, "to the novitiate that the novices may profit by it, and that the novice-father may keep it carefully as a treasure of which I myself have not known how to make good use. I entreat of those who read it to pray to God for a sinner who, having such a precious mine at his disposal, instead of drawing from it the pure gold of sanctity, has collected nothing but its rust."

Cartagena, which was founded by Pedro de Heredia in 1533, owed its great commercial importance to its superb harbor. It is situated in the Caribbean Sea near the most northerly point of South America, to the east of the Isthmus of Panama. It is in the tropics, about seven hundred miles north of the Equator.

When Peter Claver first set foot in Cartagena, he kissed the ground, which was to be the scene of his future labors. He had every reason to rejoice, for the climate of Cartagena was disagreeably hot and moist, the country around was flat and marshy, the soil was barren, the necessities of life had to be imported, and in the time of Peter Claver, fresh vegetables were almost unknown. In the seventeenth century, Cartagena was the happy hunting ground of fever-bearing insects from tropical swamps. These, the natural disadvantages of Cartagena, might have been wasted on a robust saint, but Claver must have been consoled to feel that the fine edge of these discomforts would not be blunted by a naturally healthy constitution. He had, indeed, been warned that delicate health might easily succumb to excessive heat.

Cartagena was the chief center for the slave trade. Slave traders picked up slaves at four crowns a head on the coast of Guinea or Congo and sold them for two hundred crowns or more at Cartagena. Lest the reader be tempted to raise the cry of "profiteer," it is only just to remember that the voyage lasted two months, slaves cannot live on air, even foul air, and that the overheads may fairly be credited with 33 percent or so of slaves who died en route. Further, when we take into consideration the low esteem in which the honorable profession of slave trading has always been held, we cannot consider that the profits, though large, were excessive.

Of the ten thousand slaves or so who were landed annually at Cartagena, the slaves of Guinea were the best, the blackest, and the most courageous. They were called "the Negroes of good alloy," and their one defect was a "stupid pride," to quote a contemporary writer, which made them unreasonably intractable. Against this, the slaves of Angola and Congo were mild and amenable. They accepted Christianity with the greatest fervor. Indeed, those who had been baptized were in the habit of joining the ranks of those who were to receive the sacrament in the hopes of being baptized again, inspired, no doubt, by the not unnatural belief that one could not have too much of a good thing.

Claver, on his return to Cartagena, discovered that the Jesuits had been obliged to leave their house. The new house was well adapted to satisfy Claver's zeal for mortification. It was situated between a slaughter house and a noisy tavern, whence issued the profane songs customary in such places. Moreover, the Jesuits had to live on alms, and when alms were not forthcoming, they lived on air. "These united trials," observed Fr. Fleuriau, "sufficed to make the residence delightful to the new missioners."

Fr. Claver, whose life's work was to be the instruction, the conversion, and the care of the slaves who landed in Cartagena, began his ministry under the guidance of Fr. Alfonso de Sandoval, whose career has already been described in chapter 8.

Fr. Claver never experienced that momentary weakness that always overcame the heroic Sandoval when a slave ship was announced. The horror with which Sandoval contemplated a return to these scenes of squalid misery only serves to increase our admiration of the courage with which he conquered these very natural shrinkings of the flesh.

Fr. Claver, on the other hand, was transported with joy when messengers announced the arrival of a fresh cargo of Africans. Indeed, he bribed the officials of Cartagena with the promise to say Mass for the intentions of whoever was first to bring him this joyful news. But there was no need for such bribes, for among the simple pleasures of life must be counted the happiness of bringing good news to a grateful recipient. The governor himself coveted this mission, for the happiness of watching the radiant dawn of joy on the saint's face. At the words "Another slave ship," his eyes brightened, and color flooded back into his pale, emaciated cheeks.

In the intervals between the arrival of slave ships, Fr. Claver wandered round the town with a sack. He went from house to house, begging for little comforts for the incoming cargo. Claver enjoyed the respect of the responsible officials of the Crown in Cartagena, devout Catholics who approved warmly the work of instruction that the good Father carried on among the slaves. They felt this responsibility for the welfare of these exiles. Such opposition as Claver encountered among the Spaniards came from the traders and planters, who were often inconvenienced by Claver's zeal on behalf of his black children.

The black cargo arrived in a condition of pitiable terror. They were convinced that they were to be bought by merchants who needed their fat to grease the keels of ships, and their blood to dye the sails, for this was one of the favorite bedtime stories with which they had been regaled by friendly mariners during the two months' passage.

The first appearance of Fr. Claver was often greeted with screams of terror, but it was only a matter of moments to convince these frantic creatures that Claver was no purchaser of slave fat and slave blood. He scarcely needed the interpreters who accompanied him for this purpose, for the language of love survived in the confusion of Babel and readily translated itself into gesture. *Cor ad cor loquitur.* Long before the interpreters had finished explaining that the story that had so terrified them was the invention of the devil, Fr. Claver had already soothed and comforted them by his very presence. And not only by his presence, for Claver was a practical evangelist. The biscuits, brandy, tobacco, and lemons that he distributed were practical tokens of friendship. "We must," he said, "speak to them with our hands, before we try to speak to them with our lips."

After a brief talk to the black slaves on deck, Claver descended to the sick between decks. In this work, he was often alone. Many of his African interpreters were unable to endure the stench and fainted at the first contact with that appalling atmosphere. Claver, however, did not recoil. Indeed, he regarded this part of his work as of special importance. Again and again he was able to impart to some poor dying wretch those elements of Christian truth that justified him in administering Baptism.

It is recorded that the person of Fr. Claver was sometimes illumined with rays of glory as he passed through the hospital wards of Cartagena. It may well be that a radiance no less illuminating lit the dark bowels of the slave ship as Fr. Claver moved among the dying. There they lay in the slime, the stench, and the gloom, their bodies still bleeding from the lash, their souls still suffering from insults and contempt. There they lay and, out of the depths, called upon the tribal gods who had deserted them, and called in vain. Then suddenly things changed. The dying Africans saw a face bending over them, a face illumined with love, and a voice infinitely tender, and the deft movement of kind hands easing their tortured bodies, and — supreme miracle — his lips meeting their filthy sores in a kiss. A love so divine was an unconquerable argument for the God in whom Fr. Claver believed.

When Fr. Claver returned next day, he was welcomed with ecstatic cries of childlike affection.

Two or three days usually passed before arrangements at the port could be completed to allow the disembarkation of a fresh cargo of slaves. When the day of disembarkation arrived, Fr. Claver was always present, waiting on shore with another stock of provisions and delicacies. Sometimes he would carry the sick ashore in his own arms. Again and again in the records of his mission, we find evidences of his strength, which seemed almost supernatural. His diet would have been ridiculously inadequate for a normal man living a sedentary life. His neglect of sleep would have killed a normal man within a few years, but in spite of his contempt for all ordinary rules of health, in spite of a constitution that was none too strong at the outset of his career, he proved himself capable of outworking and outwalking and outnursing all his colleagues. He made every effort to secure for the sick special carts, as otherwise they ran the risk of being driven forward under the lash. He did not leave them until he had seen them to their lodgings, and men said that Fr. Claver escorting slaves back to Cartagena reminded them of a conqueror entering Rome in triumph.

It was after the slaves had been lodged in the magazines where they awaited their sale and ultimate disposal that Claver's real work began. In the case of the dying, Claver was satisfied if he could awaken some dim sense of contrition of sin, and some faint glimmering of understanding of the fundamental Christian belief. The healthy slaves, however, had to qualify by a course of rigid instruction for the privilege of Baptism.

I have already referred to the crowded conditions of the compound in which the slaves were stocked on disembarkation, and to the squalor and misery that was the result of the infectious diseases from which many of them were suffering. The stink of sick slaves, confined in a limited space, often proved insupportable to Fr. Claver's black interpreters. It was in this noxious and empoisoned air that Peter Claver's greatest work was achieved.

A Saint in the Slave Trade

Before the day's work began, Fr. Claver prepared himself by special prayers before the Blessed Sacrament and by self-inflicted austerities. He then passed through the streets of Cartagena, accompanied by his African interpreters and bearing a staff crowned by a cross. On his shoulder he carried a bag that contained his stole and surplice, the necessities for the arrangements of an altar, and his little store of comforts and delicacies. Heavily loaded though he was, his companions found it difficult to keep up with this eager little man who dived through the crowded streets with an enthusiasm that suggested a lover hurrying to a trysting place.

His first care on arrival was for the sick. He had a delicacy of touch in the cleansing and dressing of sores that was a true expression of his personality. After he had made the sick comfortable on their couches and given them a little wine and brandy and refreshed them with scented water, he then proceeded to collect the healthier slaves into an open space.

In his work of instruction, Claver relied freely on pictures. This method appealed effectively to the simple African mind and was, moreover, in accordance with the teachings of his order, for, as we have seen, St. Ignatius in his Spiritual Exercises was constant in urging the exercitant to picture to himself sensibly the subject matter of his meditations. His favorite picture was in the form of a triptych: In the center, Christ on the Cross, His precious blood flowing from each wound into a vase; below the Cross, a priest collecting this blood to baptize a faithful black man. On the right side of the triptych, a naively dramatic group of Africans, glorious and splendidly arrayed; on the left side, the wicked Africans, hideous and deformed, surrounded by unlovely monsters.

Claver was particularly careful to make every possible arrangement for the comfort of his catechumens. He himself remained standing, even in the heat of the day, and the slave masters, who sometimes attended these edifying ceremonies, often remonstrated with the slaves for remaining seated while their instructor stood. But Fr. Claver always intervened and explained with great earnestness to the slave masters that the slaves were the really important people at this particular performance, and that he himself was a mere cipher who was there for their convenience. Sometimes, if a slave was so putrescent with sores as to be revolting to his neighbors and, worse still, to prevent them from concentrating their thoughts on Fr. Claver's instruction, he would throw his cloak over him as a screen. Again, he would often use his cloak as a cushion for the infirm. On such occasions, the cloak was often withdrawn so infected and filthy as to require most drastic cleansing. Fr. Claver, however, was so engrossed in his work that he would have resumed his cloak immediately had not his interpreters forcibly prevented him.

This cloak was to serve many purposes during his ministry: as a veil to disguise repulsive wounds, as a shield for leprous and lupus-ravaged black slaves, as a pall for those who had died, as a pillow for the sick. The cloak was soon to acquire a legendary fame. Its very touch cured the sick and revived the dying. Men fought to come into contact with it, to tear fragments from it as relics. Indeed, before long its edge was ragged with torn shreds.

It was Fr. Claver's custom to present each black man and woman on Baptism with a leaden medal bearing the names of Jesus and Mary. Some such mark of identification was important, for one of his great difficulties was the fact that many Africans who professed Christianity had never been baptized. Many Africans had been smuggled into the country to avoid the government tax, and years might pass before Fr. Claver established contact with them. Slaves who had been resident in the colony for many years often acquired familiarity with Christian usages and were in the habit of attending divine service.

Now, snobbery is the most endemic of human feelings, and the slave who had acquired this thin veneer of Christian culture regarded himself as being infinitely superior, socially and otherwise, to the new arrivals from Africa. A revivalist at Eton who expected the Captain of the Boats to attend the same prayer meeting as a new boy would probably meet with indifferent success. And it required all Fr. Claver's tact to persuade the residents among the Africans who had never been baptized to put in an appearance when he was instructing Africans who had just landed in Cartagena.

Fr. Claver made no easy appeal to religious emotion. The contrast between the rationalism of St. Thomas Aquinas and the uninstructed emotionalism of Gipsy Smith was no greater than the contrast between the methods of Fr. Claver and the technique of Welsh revivalists. Fr. Claver would have distrusted those transports of emotion that are the product of a mass conviction of spiritual salvation. All his efforts were concentrated on appealing to the uncultivated intelligence rather than to the unlimited emotions of the African. Slowly and surely, the slaves were encouraged to make the mental effort necessary to grasp in outline, at least, the profound spiritual truths. Claver never lost his patience or permitted himself to be discouraged by the queer misconstructions that dull or fanciful Africans put upon the lessons that he taught. He was versatile in the methods that he employed to conquer their dull intelligences. We have seen the use that he made of pictures. Where pictures failed, he would use analogy and gesture. To illustrate, for instance, the efficacy of the sacrament of Baptism, he would say, "My children, we must be like the serpent, which throws off its old skin to receive another more beautiful and more brilliant," and he would draw his nails across his hand as though tearing off the skin. His pupils would be urged to imitate this gesture in order to prove that they had understood the point that he was trying to make.

Even in his most elementary instruction, Fr. Claver never forgot his aim, not merely to transform heathens into nominal Christians but to convert nominal into real Christians. He devoted all his energies to the task of awakening in these wretched men a lively sense of sin and a determination to lead lives of real devotion to Christ. The slave yard, as I have already said, resounded with the wailings of contrite sinners, as he held up the crucifix before their eyes, calling upon them to make an act of contrition.

Claver's work was not confined to Cartagena. Cartagena was a slave mart, and very few slaves whom Fr. Claver baptized in Cartagena remained there. Now, Fr. Claver was determined not to lose his converts, and it was therefore his practice to conduct a series of country missions after Easter. He went from village to village, crossing mountain ranges, traversing swamps and bogs, making his way through forests. On arriving in a village, he would plant a cross in the marketplace, and there he would await the sunset and the return from the fields of the slaves whom he had first met — it might be some weeks, it might be some years — before in Cartagena. The ecstatic welcome that marked these scenes of reunion were a royal recompense for the hardships of the missionary journey.

Fr. Claver never lost his ascendancy over the men whom he had baptized. On one occasion, a mere message from him was sufficient to arrest the flight of a panic-stricken African population retreating in disorder from a volcano in eruption. Fr. Claver's messenger stopped the rout, and Fr. Claver's bodily presence the next day transformed a terror-infected mob into a calm and orderly procession that followed him without fear round the very edge of the still active crater, on the crest of which Fr. Claver planted a triumphant cross.

Though Fr. Claver's activities were not confined, as we shall soon see, to the slaves, the "slave of the slaves" regarded himself as, above all, consecrated to their service. Proud Spaniards who sought him out had to be content with such time as he could spare from the ministrations of the slaves. This attitude did not meet with universal approval. Spanish ladies complained that the smell of the slaves who had attended Fr. Claver's daybreak Mass clung tenaciously to the church and rendered its interior insupportable to sensitive nostrils for the remainder of the day. How could they possibly be expected to confess to Fr. Claver in a confessional used by slaves and impregnated with their presence? "I quite agree," replied Fr. Claver, with the disarming simplicity of the saint. "I am not the proper confessor for fine ladies. You should go to some other confessor. My confessional was never meant for ladies of quality. It is too narrow for their gowns. It is only suited to poor Negro women."

But were his Spanish ladies satisfied with this reply? Not a bit. It was Fr. Claver to whom they wished to confess, and if the worst had come to the worst, they were prepared to use the same confessional as the slave women. "Very well, then," replied Fr. Claver, meekly, "but I am afraid you must wait until all my Negro women have been absolved."

In the sight of God, the white man and the black man may be equal, but in the sight of Fr. Claver, the black man had precedence every time.

But fashionable people have souls, and Fr. Claver was always prepared to do what he could for people of quality if they were in serious distress or in disgrace. But in all other cases, as his biographer, Fr. Fleuriau, tells us, he tried civilly to get rid of them, because much time must be lost with them in compliments, ceremony, and useless or worldly discourse, whilst he only cared to speak of God.

Fr. Claver would have heartily sympathized with this entry in John Wesley's *Journal:* "I dined at Lady _____'s. We need great grace to converse with great people. From which, therefore (unless in rare instances), I am glad to be excused. Of these two hours I can give no account." But though Fr. Claver's love for the slaves knew no bounds, his love was not only for the slave as a class, but he had a strong affection for individual slaves. There was nothing weak or soft in his attitude to these unstable converts.

African dances often degenerated into unrestrained orgies. These orgies were often interrupted by the impetuous invasion of Fr. Claver, adequately armed with a crucifix and a scourge with which he struck both dancers and musicians. "The instruments," writes Fr. Fleuriau, "which were quickly abandoned, he took possession of as trophies wrested from the devil; he confided them to the care of some zealous Christian with the order not to restore them till the owners had bestowed some alms on the poor in the lepers' hospital."

Fr. Claver never hesitated to exploit the most theatrical devices as a means of arousing contrition in the African breast. His technique, for instance, of dealing with drunkards was impressively dramatic. The drunkard was made to lick the ground with his tongue — a curious remedy that might have been expected to aggravate rather than to quench the penitent's thirst — and to complete the picture, Fr. Claver placed his foot lightly on the offender's neck, exclaiming, "Who art thou, miserable creature, that darest thus attack Heaven and outrage the divine majesty?"

A Saint in the Slave Trade

That, of course, is the kind of question for which it would be difficult to frame an adequate reply if one were standing upon one's feet, and quite impossible if one's nose is in the process of being firmly pressed into the dust.

11

Claver and the Whites

Fr. Claver's work was not confined to slaves. For weeks together, no slave ship might land in Cartagena, and at such times, Fr. Claver found abundant occupation in the hospitals, in the prisons, and among the social derelicts at Cartagena.

In one such interval, he was appointed Father Minister of the Jesuit College — an important office. Fr. Claver was distressed by this appointment, for the last thing that this "slave of the slaves" desired was to be placed in a position of authority over his brethren. He accepted the position only "under obedience" and promptly proceeded to enslave himself to those over whom he had been placed in authority. He swept the filthiest parts of the house, begged the cook to give him the most disagreeable jobs, a request that the cook obligingly granted, and, in general, insisted on doing the work of all his subordinates. It is useless to place in command a man whose only ambition is to obey, and before long he was exempted from his post of Father Minister in order to be entrusted with new, onerous, and hardly less inappropriate duties.

Cartagena at this period attracted the sort of adventurer who in more recent times found his way out to the goldfields of South Africa. The percentage of failures among such men was greater than the percentage of successes, and many of these social derelicts, having failed in this life, decided to put their shirt on the next. And provided with little more than this shirt, they besieged the religious orders and demanded to be admitted. Their qualifications for the priesthood were unimpressive, and the best that could be done with them was to found a special order of lay brothers at Cartagena of which Fr. Claver was put in charge.

Fr. Claver proved to be a bewildering novice master. At one moment, he would be waiting on these novices with disconcerting humility, and at the next, he would be dragooning them into tasks of self-abnegation imposed in all good faith to confirm their souls in virtue. He would, for instance, lead them through the streets with brooms in their hands to the hospitals, where they would be expected not only to make the beds of the patients but to perform the most menial services for the most infected slaves. At other times, he would fill an enormous basket with provisions. This basket would be supported on a pole, to one end of which Fr. Claver attached himself and to the other end of which he attached an unwilling lay brother. I have already commented on Fr. Claver's superhuman strength when engaged in missionary activities. Even the youngest and most robust of the lay brothers often collapsed with exhaustion on such occasions. The heaviest of provision baskets seemed to make no difference to Fr. Claver, as he galloped on ahead, oblivious of the muttered imprecations that came from the other end of the pole.

At other times he invited his lay brothers to lend their cloaks to the slaves to be used as cushions or to cover the wounds and ulcers of the sick.

Much of Fr. Claver's time was spent with the Dutch and English prisoners of war. He did not find the Mohammedans easy to convert, but even with them he was often successful. Among the English he made one notable convert.

Six hundred English prisoners of war had been taken after the recapture of the islands of St. Christopher and St. Catherine by the Spaniards. Fr. Claver was asked to say Mass on the flagship and was invited to a dinner at which the English officers were the guests of their Spanish captors. Fr. Claver accepted this invitation in the hope of establishing contact with men who might thus be converted to the Catholic Faith.

He made such a favorable impression on the English officers that they insisted on introducing him to the archdeacon of London, who had been visiting these islands when they were captured. The captain tentatively suggested that Fr. Claver might not object to falling in with English customs and might even be prepared to drink the archdeacon's health. Fr. Claver agreed. Jesus Christ, he reminded himself, had drunk with publicans; His follower might, to win souls, drink to an archdeacon. The venerable old gentleman with a long gray beard was then introduced into the cabin. Toasts were exchanged, and the archdeacon asked in Latin for a private interview. Fr. Claver, perceiving that the archdeacon was none too happy in his heresy, opened the ball by reminding the archdeacon that the day was the feast day of "an illustrious virgin, the honor of your country." St. Ursula, the feast they were celebrating, was the daughter of St. Lucius, a British king, whom Fr. Claver described as "the model of a truly Christian king," for the excellent reason that this truly Christian king "sent annually to the Holy See presents worthy of a monarch." Fr. Claver then proceeded with a few telling strokes to point the contrast by a word picture of Henry VIII. "Shall the authority of a king," he asked, "notorious for vice, outweigh that of so many others distinguished for their piety? Can the religion introduced by the piety of a Lucius be false and the one founded on the adultery of a Henry be true? If this Prince could not sustain his new crimes but by the support of a new religion, why must you, who are not guilty of the same crimes, adhere to this same religion?"

The archdeacon sighed gently, and made the surprising admission that it was only the fear of poverty and the fact that he had a wife and children to support that prevented him from repudiating Henry VIII and all his works. He insisted, however, that he would die, if he could, a Catholic. "Pray for me, Father," he said between his tears, "pray earnestly."

Weeks passed, and then one day, on a visit to the hospital of St. Sebastian, Fr. Claver met a closed litter. It was the archdeacon, dying, but sufficiently master of himself to remember and to keep his promise. He died a Catholic.

Many of the English prisoners of war followed him into the Church.

Fr. Claver's hospital work was divided between St. Sebastian's, the hospital for general cases, and St. Lazarus's, for the lepers. In both hospitals he undertook with joy the most menial and degraded duties that could be found for him. It was commonly said in Cartagena that Fr. Claver did the work of forty workmen. His return to these hospitals after a temporary absence was a signal for great rejoicing. The patients accorded him a kind of public triumph.

But perhaps his noblest work was done among the lepers. Among my readers there must be many who have never seen a leper and who will therefore find it difficult to understand the horror that lepers inspire. I shall never forget my first sight of a leper in the East, a momentary, terrifying glimpse. To touch a leper is a test of courage; to tend his wounds, a test of heroism.

On one occasion, a Spanish officer met Claver beyond the town wall. On observing his cheerful expression, he asked him where he was going. "I am going," answered Claver, "to keep my carnival with my poor at St. Lazarus's." The Spaniard followed him out of curiosity. On arriving at the church door, Claver collected all the lepers who could still walk, and seating himself on a stone, he heard their confessions, wrapping his cloak round them, as the weather was cold.

There are degrees of leprosy, and there are lepers whose appearance is so terrible that they form an outer circle of outcasts in the inferno of leprosy. They are shunned by other lepers just as lepers are shunned by other men. Claver would seek out these abandoned wretches in the secluded cells in which they were confined, and he would, in the words of his biographer, "handle their wounds with as much complacency as if they had been the most delicate flowers; he tenderly kissed them, and even wiped them with his tongue. He washed those who could not use their arms, he fed them, and if he saw anyone disgusted with the food, he would take a piece out of the dish and eat it himself in order to encourage the invalid."

Do not make the mistake of believing that Claver was insensitive or that these demonstrations of extravagant love for the least lovable of God's creatures cost him nothing. We shall see, in due course, that they cost him a great deal.

Fr. Claver did not confine himself to gestures or to prayers. He was an exponent of that practical Christianity of which we hear so much from people who are neither practical nor Christian. He did everything in his power to mitigate the misery of these poor wretches. He collected material for mosquito curtains, had it stitched into shape by a slave woman, and himself placed the curtains in position. He never went to St. Lazarus's without an abundant supply of linen, perfumes, bandages, and other remedies. No surgeon dared approach these lepers to bleed them, but Fr. Claver somehow managed to secure a stock of lancets and taught the lepers to bleed each other.

"One loving heart," says St. Augustine, "sets another on fire." Though lesser mortals were able to follow Fr. Claver only at a respectable distance, he did succeed in coaxing occasional musicians to accompany him to the hospitals, where they would perform for the benefit of an audience that they hardly dared to look at. Never did musicians keep their eyes so sedulously glued to the score.

Fr. Claver spent a great deal of time in prison cells, consoling criminals under sentence of death. Such was the potency of his influence that the most savage of criminals were often induced by him to supplement the penalties that they had incurred with self-inflicted penances.

He accompanied the criminals to the gallows, heartened them with brandy as they climbed the ladder, wiped their wet foreheads with his handkerchief, and held them tenderly while the rope was being fixed, perhaps not too tenderly, round their necks.

A priest incurs "irregularity" if he is in anyway directly concerned with the carrying out of capital punishment, but not if he is solely occupied in consoling the criminal. *Irregularity* is a technical term, and those who incur "irregularity" are incapable of receiving Holy Orders unless dispensed, or of exercising any Holy Orders that they have received.

There is a story that turns on this point, a story that illustrates the perpetual contrast between the spirit and the letter. A Spanish captain had been condemned to the flames for coining false money. He was to be strangled before being thrown to the flames, but the rope broke at the first turn. Claver caught the poor wretch in his arms and pressed his face against his own while the hangman passed another rope round his neck. The cord broke a second time, and a pedantic Pharisee who was standing by exclaimed that Claver had incurred "irregularity" and could no longer exercise his priestly functions, since the executioner's rope had touched him in falling.

"Well, be it so," answered Claver, "if at this price I can save a soul."

Claver had no sooner defied the letter than he realized that he had the letter on his side, that the pedant was wrong, as pedants frequently are wrong, and that, in point of fact, he had incurred no "irregularity." With unwonted asperity, he told the man not to talk nonsense. Once again Claver pressed the man's hideously distorted face against his own until at last the poor wretch died.

In the condemned cell was found a prayer book, in which the man who was to die had written a few words after Fr. Claver had visited him: "This book belongs to the happiest man in the world."

12

Servus Servorum

The heroism that finds expression in sudden, unpremeditated acts of self-sacrifice may be more dramatic but not more impressive than the undaunted perseverance in drudgery unredeemed by romance. Claver knew exactly what he was in for when he sealed his profession with the words "*Petrus Claver aethiopum semper servus.*" He had been at work for six years when he vowed to be the slave of the Ethiopians forever.

Forever ... The task to which he had consecrated his life was a task without end, a labor of perpetual beginning. "Always," as Fr. Martindale says, "he had to go back to the start of things; and after rowing, as it were, a few strokes forward, he must needs find that the stream had swept him back to his starting place. Faces passed and passed before him until his life must have felt, at times, a mere shadow pantomime."

It was heartbreaking work. First there was the difficulty of language. He learned Angola, the commonest dialect, but he had to employ numerous interpreters to help him out. Of these interpreters, one spoke four languages, but as there were sometimes as many as forty dialects in the same slave ship, it is not surprising that in some cases one African slave alone might require a chain of five interpreters, each speaking different dialects. Think for a moment of the immense difficulty of explaining the Atonement through a chain of slaves to some poor outcast of feeble intelligence who would have had the greatest difficulty in understanding the simplest Christian doctrine even if conveyed to him directly by one of his own people.

Fr. Claver's day's work began with a little honest charring. He began by scrubbing the floorboards of the confessional to protect the slaves from the damp and from the stench that the wood might have contracted. In Lent, he would enter his confessional at three in the morning and would remain there for eight hours, listening to a constant succession of slaves. After eight hours in the confessional, he left the church for a brief pause and returned for another four hours in the afternoon.

And throughout these incredible labors, he wore a hair shirt that reached from his neck to his feet. Sometimes he fainted from exhaustion, but he usually managed to avoid collapse by wiping his face with linen steeped in wine. In Lent, his only meal in the day consisted of a piece of coarse bread and some fried potatoes in the evening. On retiring to his room, he rounded off his day by scourging himself, and of the remainder of the night, he spent at least two hours in mental prayer.

He seems never to have touched meat, green vegetables, or fruit, and our moderns who cannot exist without vitamins may explain, if they can, why Fr. Claver never once contracted scurvy, an endemic complaint among sailors deprived of fresh fruit and vegetables.

The miracles of healing that were attributed to him are less astonishing than the fact that this incredible energy was maintained for thirty-eight years on a daily average of three hours' sleep and—for food—a few pieces of bread and fried potatoes.

Once a lay brother gathered a fine bunch of grapes and offered it to Claver and was much vexed when Claver declined the gift. Seeing that he was hurt, Claver ate two grapes and remarked that they were the first grapes that he had ever tasted in America.

There are many facts that reinforce the belief that Fr. Claver drew on a supernatural source of energy. During his novitiate, he was peculiarly sensitive to heat. Indeed, while studying at Santa Fe, he could never cross the court without screening his head from the intensity of the sun, but once he had fairly embarked on his missionary activities at Cartagena, he never seemed to feel the terrible heat of South America. Others, again, might be half dead with thirst before they had said an early Mass. Fr. Claver's Mass was always at noon, and though he had often been at work for eight or even nine hours before the midday Mass, he never complained of thirst.

He was even prepared, if need be, to sacrifice the one luxury that he permitted himself—his privacy. A certain slave was suffering from some hideous disease that made his very presence in a room unbearable, even to the other slaves. Fr. Claver insisted on lodging him in his own room and giving him his own bed. Daily he carried him his food, washed him and dressed his wounds, and slept contentedly on the floor at the foot of the bed.

That this act of abnegation was a real sacrifice is clear from another incident. The Father Rector of the Jesuit House at Cartagena often came to Fr. Claver for confession after Claver had retired for the night, and thereby provoked the only complaint Fr. Claver is known to have made in these eight-and-thirty years. "At least," pleaded the saint, "at least leave me the night or choose some other confessor."

Fully to appreciate a life such as St. Peter Claver's, it is necessary to use, if only in a modified form, the method of the Spiritual Exercises. We should not be content merely to read the story of his heroic endurances. We should try, in the Ignatian manner, to make that record live. We should force ourselves to see with the eyes of the mind the loathsome and corrupted bodies of the lepers whose wounds he kissed. We should try to re-create in imagination the stench of the compound in which the African slaves lay. Indeed, all our senses should be enlisted in this reconstruction. The sense of sound as we recall the groans of the dying slaves, the sense of taste when we remember that Fr. Claver picked up a morsel of food which a sick slave had refused to swallow and had spat out on the table, and ate it himself with apparent relish to encourage these slaves to try again, and finally the sense of touch. Great paintings are said to possess tactile value when they stimulate our sense of touch. Surely the record of Claver's work must possess this tactile value for those who force themselves, if only in imagination, to bring their lips into contact with the wounds which Claver kissed.

But in this pain-dreading age, the Ignatian method is out of fashion. Indeed, people pride themselves rather on a squeamishness that hurriedly turns from an age that records such horrors. I, for one, read only with the greatest difficulty the tales of tortures inflicted on martyrs, whereas if I were a true disciple of St. Ignatius, I should do my best to reconstruct every incident of the torture chamber.

There is, indeed, no cause for self-satisfaction in the shrinking from the mere thought of horrors that brave men endured without complaint. Though we rightly condemn the depraved taste that feeds on horrors, actual or recorded, we need not condone the pain-dreading temper that shrinks even from the thought of suffering.

The Spanish lady who forced herself to watch Fr. Claver in his work struck the right note when she explained to her daughter,

"See that holy man kissing wounds that we scarcely venture to look at." This lady drew the only possible moral: "Is it not shameful for us to do nothing for the service of our brethren?"

Fr. Claver's example, we are told, "gave courage to the most delicate." May the record of his life steel the "most delicate" of his admirers not only to read but also to reconstruct in imagination the more repulsive incidents chronicled in these pages.

"True humanity," as Charles James Fox remarked in the course of a debate on the slave trade in the House of Commons, "consists not in a squeamish ear; it consists not in starting or shrinking at such tales as these, but in a disposition of heart to relieve misery. True humanity appertains rather to the mind than to the nerves, and prompts men to use real and active endeavors to execute the actions which it suggests."

It is tempting to search for some belittling clue to conduct that shames us by its heroism. It would be reassuring if we could lessen the gulf between Claver and our own self-indulgent selves by striving to believe that he enjoyed kissing sores because he was crudely insensitive to dirt and filth. But the facts do not support this consoling hypothesis. The self-inflicted penances that our moderns find so difficult to condone were designed, among other things, to subdue the natural shrinking of the body from repulsive sound and smell, but there were moments when even the heroic Claver shrank.

He was once called to the house of a merchant to hear the confession of a slave who was so ulcerous and infected that he had been thrown into a remote corner to save others from his insupportable presence. Claver recoiled when he saw (and smelled) this miserable man. Then, overwhelmed with remorse for his cowardice, he retired into a corner, flogged himself severely for this failure of nerves, and returned to the slave and, as evidence of his contrition, kissed his wounds and applied his tongue to the more repulsive sores on the slave's body.

It would be easier to understand this supreme demonstration of the love that no horrors can dim if this kissing of sores or sucking poison out of envenomed wounds was an isolated, unpremeditated gesture. The uncharitable might even suspect the faint suggestion of a stunt, designed for display, in a unique instance of such dramatic self-conquest. Claver made a regular practice of this sort of thing, and I think he was inspired by two distinct motives.

In the first place, he was acutely conscious of the need to restore self-respect to those whose very presence inspired normal people with disgust. And when he kissed their wounds, the very extravagance of this gesture must have helped to convince the ulcerous lepers and infected slaves of the difficult truth that man is made in the image of God and that the most degraded of lepers is infinitely precious in the eyes of God and in the eyes of God's saints.

In the second place, Claver was fighting the battle that never ended between his higher and his lower self, between his soul and that other part of him that shrank, as we all shrink, from disgusting sights and smells. And he knew that these instinctive shrinkings, these natural movements of the flesh, could be conquered only if he treated them roughly. If he once allowed them to gain the upper hand, his mission might end in failure.

But though he steeled himself to ignore the most revolting smells and sights when he alone was inconvenienced, he remained to the last delicately sensitive to the feelings of his less austere companions, and he strove, for their sakes, when he was accompanied, to mitigate in every way, with smelling salts and scented waters, the frightful stench in which they worked.

And though he just did not see filth when recognition of its presence would have impeded his work, he protected the

Sacrament by silken veils from all possibility of contamination as he carried it with infinite care to the hospital or slave sheds.

Claver's life was a miracle of love. He translated into action one of the most difficult of Christian doctrines, the doctrine that God loves every individual soul. The romantic criminal and the practitioner of mean and squalid vices, the brilliant and the half-witted, the gross and the sinful, the slave owner no less than the slave, the self-indulgent, the squalid, the dreary, the bores, yes, even the crashing bores, God loves them all. A hard saying.

And that is, perhaps, one of the reasons why God gives us saints and has endowed His saints with the divine power of loving the unlovable.

And indeed, it was only a love supernatural in its motive that could possibly have sustained Claver through the mean drudgery of those thirty-eight years. There was, no doubt, a touch of romance in the kiss with which he sealed his pity for the hideous wounds, but there was nothing romantic in the visits he continued to pay for fourteen years to an old slave broken down by age and illness, who had been abandoned in a miserable hut outside the city walls. Week by week, he visited this wretched slave, brought him food and delicacies, made his bed, tended his wounds, and consoled him in his sorrows.

Fourteen years. Not a job for which many Christians would volunteer with enthusiasm.

There is nothing in the least romantic about nursing slaves suffering from the most prosaic of diseases, violent dysentery. Such, at least, was the decided view of a slave woman, Magdalen de Mendoza, whom Claver had persuaded to accompany him to the sheds where these men lay. He took one of these slaves into his arms, and the wretched man covered Claver with infectious filth. The stench was so appalling that the woman was overcome and fled in panic from the room. Claver rushed after her. "Magdalen, Magdalen," he exclaimed, "for God's sake, come back! Have you forgotten that these men are our brothers, our brothers, every one of whom has been redeemed by our Lord's own Blood?" What indeed could be plainer? One can imagine the ring of astonishment in his voice. Saints are like that. They always act with this shattering conviction on the beliefs that we others so half-heartedly hold. The failure of ordinary people to implement without hesitation the conclusions that follow so irresistibly from the Christian premise is a source of never-ending and staggering astonishment to the saint. Claver was genuinely at a loss to explain the bewildering fact that mere filth and stench had overpowered the love that every Christian must feel for the least lovable of those for whom Christ died. "Can't you understand, Magdalen? These men, these Negroes lying in their filth, are our *brothers*. Our brothers, for whom Christ died."

Magdalen understood. His amazement struck her like a whip. She was shamed into returning. And down the corridors of time we, too, can hear the echoes of his great surprise.

To the modern, the excessive humility of St. Peter Claver must seem as unattractive as his love of suffering. It is easy to suspect the sincerity of holy men who continue to harp on their sins, easy to believe that the saint is anxious to emphasize still further the gulf that separates him from sinners. And if this theory were true, the saint's attitude might be represented as follows: "I who am holy register the most edifying and exaggerated con-trition for the most trivial of sins. You who are sinful are quite complacently self-satisfied. You, who ought to be ashamed of yourself, are proud, and I, who have every reason to be proud, add humility to my other virtues."

Let us see if we can suggest an alternative explanation of the saint's perplexing humility. In the first place, humility must not be confused with mere modesty, particularly with the superficial modesty that is derived from manners rather than from mind.

Thought is free, and society would be impossible if we were forever conducting inquisitions into motives and intentions. Overt action alone must be the test. So, in this matter of modesty, it is tacitly agreed that a man may hold what view he wishes of his own virtues, provided that he does not offend against good manners by inflicting self-praise upon others.

The savage who has established his claim to preeminence by defeating his rivals is permitted to blow his own trumpet with great vigor. As civilization advances, the technique of the trumpet becomes more and more civilized. Society evolves a ritual of modesty. The ritualistic compliment must be met by the ritualistic response. Not only the words, but the tone and gesture for the acknowledgment of a compliment are all standardized. Intention does not matter, for modesty is deemed to be valid if the form and matter are correct.

The ceremonial of cricket has a place for ritualistic modesty. A cricketer, for instance, who has made fifty, starts back to the pavilion at his normal walking pace. He begins to run as the clapping grows in volume and breaks into a smart gallop as he approaches the pavilion steps. But this concession to ceremonial throws no light whatever on the question as to whether a cricketer is modest or vain. Those who are delighted and those who are embarrassed by public ovations react in precisely the same way to the cheers of the spectators.

No doubt mistakes are easy, for the ritual of modesty is exacting. Observe, for instance, the cricketer who has made twenty-five. Mild clapping breaks out as he approaches the pavilion. The poor man's indecision is painful. If he does not quicken his steps, people may vaguely suspect that he is attempting to spin out the precious moments during which he is the focus of cheering spectators. If, on the other hand, he breaks into a premature run, he may be accused of exaggerating the warmth and the volume of the applause.

At my own school a smart amble was considered correct for twenty-five, a quick run for fifty, but the "Heavens, I can't bear another moment of this" gallop was not permissible for anything short of a century.

Modesty is a virtue, but deliberate cultivation of the appearance of modesty is a subtle form of conceit. Subtle, since the conceit that, in effect, claims to be modest is subtler, though hardly less unpleasing, than the conceit that claims to have good cause for conceit.

Many years ago, when I first began to read the lives of the saints, I was inclined to suspect the sincerity of their self-abasement. Humility ranks high among the Christian virtues, and to claim this virtue, if only by implication, is as objectionable, so I felt, as to lay claim to any other virtue. The man of true humility must therefore be careful to avoid making any statement that, by implication, is the equivalent to laying claim to humility. We thus reach the paradoxical position that self-abasement may be the subtlest form of self-praise. Even on the most charitable construction, self-abasement may be nothing more, so I felt, than ritualistic humility analogous to the ritualistic modesty of the cricketer.

But the more I read about the saints, the more convinced I became that this first impression was absurdly superficial. I require no convincing that Fr. Claver was sincere when he stated that he ate his bread without earning it, that he was only maintained out of charity, that he should always be the first woken up for a sick call, since the others worked hard—"as for me, I do nothing at all"; or when he explained his pleasure in talking to slaves as a kind of secret pride by pointing out that uncultivated intelligences were less likely than other people to discover his weaknesses; or when he tried to deflect into jokes the praise of those who admired his self-mortification in kissing the sores of lepers, and said with a laugh, "Oh, well, if being a saint consists in having no taste and in having a strong stomach, why, I own, I may be one"; or when, in brief, he acted with complete conviction the role that he had assigned to himself, the role of the slave of the slaves.

Whatever may be the true explanation of the travesty of the truth that we find in all his own references to himself, I need waste no time in considering the possibility that Claver was insincere. His whole life was all of a piece. Humility that translates itself into action is more impressive than the humility that finds expression in words. Claver's one ambition was to act like a slave and to be treated like a slave. When he signed himself "Slave of the slaves forever," he meant exactly what he said. This was no dramatic gesture but a statement of his most obstinate intention. On his missionary journeys outside Cartagena, he placed a slave in supreme command of the party. The slave not only planned out the itinerary but arranged the details of the day's journey. On one occasion when Claver was invited to give a mission in a particular district, he replied that he would come with pleasure if his slave consented. The slave did not consent, and Claver did not go.

"Fantastic and pointless" was the comment of a friend who read the proofs of these pages. Well, there is a part of me that sympathizes with the natural reactions of the natural man to these odd manifestations of a most unnatural humility. I can also dimly understand the point of view of the saint who felt that, in taking orders from a slave, he was showing a humility that was patterned on, but still infinitely below and infinitely less than, the humility of God, who for our sakes became man and was obedient to His earthly parents.

If such was Claver's attitude to his inferiors, we need not be surprised when he exhibited extreme humility before his superiors. He would appear before his superiors like the youngest novice in the most humble attitude, "with his head uncovered, with his eyes cast down, his mind attentive to the least sign of their will."

Hence we are told by Fr. Fleuriau that his superiors never failed to throw all that was most painful upon him, being sure of meeting with no opposition, and being delighted also to get rid of the difficulty of finding people always disposed to obey.

But even the most captious critic would concede that there are, perhaps, few greater tests of humility than complete patience under the most undeserved rebuke. On one occasion, Claver, whose rapid mastery of the classics had attracted great attention during his novitiate, was attacked as an ignoramus who knew no Latin. He replied simply by acknowledging his ignorance. He did not think it necessary to qualify his reply in any way.

He was even prepared, later in life, to accept with composure the ignorant and hostile criticisms of methods whose success he had demonstrated beyond all possible doubt.

There are few things that competent people find harder to bear with good humor than the interference of incompetents in the work that they understand. Now, Claver might have been pardoned for believing himself to be the greatest living expert on the mentality of the African slave. Indeed, his astounding success in handling this very difficult material might have justified him in resenting the slightest criticism, not on his own behalf but on behalf of the slaves. Many a man who is magnanimous enough to ignore a personal affront stoutly resists any interference with the methods that he knows to be of the greatest value to those for whom he is working.

You may, indeed, criticize Claver as foolish for allowing ignorant superiors to obstruct his life's work, but you can hardly doubt the sincerity of the humility that accepted such interference without question. When, for instance, he was ordered by an unimaginative superior to abandon certain methods that had proved most fruitful in good results, he obeyed without question and said, "What a miserable creature I must be, since I cannot do a little good without occasioning a great deal of evil, and without troubling the whole house!"

Again, the following incident is characteristic. During Holy Week, Fr. Claver's eagle eye suddenly detected a lady in the congregation whose dress met with his active disapproval. I suspect that it might have been difficult to discover garments that were at once fashionable and yet capable of satisfying Fr. Claver's very exacting standards of Catholic modesty. Claver seldom passed from tacit disapproval to active censure, but on this occasion, he may have felt that the week in which Christians commemorate the agony in Gethsemane and the Crucifixion was more than usually inappropriate for a generous display of personal charms. So he descended from the pulpit and pointed out that the offending garment was not only inappropriate to Holy Week but most unsuitable in view of the lady's age. The lady would perhaps have been prepared to concede the unsuitability of the garment on the first score, but the reference to her age infuriated her, and her indignation was so noisy that the Father Sacristan hurried to the spot, expressed his active sympathy, and blamed Fr. Claver for his indiscretion.

The rector of the college happened to arrive at this moment and corrected Fr. Claver very severely as "an imprudent, indiscreet person, who without distinguishing the merits and qualifications of individuals, yielded to the impetuosity of his zeal." Whereupon Claver, uttering no word in his own defense, fell upon his knees, kissed the feet of his superior, craved pardon for the scandal that he had caused, and asked for the severest possible penance. The lady herself was most impressed and made all sorts of good resolutions.

Needless to say, many people took advantage of Claver's humility. The more ignorant slaves often treated him with great insolence, but these insults, we are told, "had inexpressible charm for him. He hearkened to them with joy that appeared in his very countenance."

Sanctity has its insoluble difficulties. No really satisfactory explanation has yet been advanced for the excesses of saintly humility. The fact that the saint is infinitely more conscious than other people of the immeasurable distance that separates the creature from his Creator no doubt explains the humility of the saint's attitude to God, but it does not explain the saint's attitude of humility to other people. Fr. Claver genuinely regarded himself as infinitely less worthy than many sinners. Was Fr. Claver sincere? Undoubtedly. What, then, is the explanation?

I have no explanation of my own to offer, but I like what Ida Coudenhove has written on this point, and perhaps the following passage from her book *The Nature of Sanctity* may help the non-Catholic reader toward a partial solution of this perplexing problem:

> Or consider the saint's *humility*—the real fear for his salvation which seems to us so superfluous, the consuming

remorse for sins which scarcely seem sins to us, the life-long tears over this and that mistake that seem to us so natural and not worth worrying about, the profound conviction of personal unworthiness, even when the rest of the world is already on its knees in reverence. Such humility seems to us mistaken, something intrinsically impossible, forced, unjust. Yes, if he were not a saint, one would detect in it the most revolting form of crooked and perverted vanity....

What then, when a man apprehends as a living reality with the whole of his startled soul the tremendous fact: that God wishes to be his friend,... that God has called him from eternity to this, to be His own, and not only that he should be God's, but, far more difficult to understand, and infinitely more difficult to believe, that God will be his ...? Do you think that that man will study moral theology to reassure himself of all the sins he has *not* committed? Can he do otherwise than remain tremblingly aware of his infinite and unalterable unworthiness, in silent adoration of a choice which he can never, never understand, but by whose reality, notwithstanding, he lives every hour of his life?

That is why the humility of the saints is so immeasurably deep, so passionate, so alert, so unforgetful, inexorable and implacable—and so fearless withal, so calm; without tormenting shame or "inferiority complex," without flight, subterfuge and contortion. For they know for sure that the Lord has taken this very Nothing that they are, this poor wretched nothing to His Heart, laid His kiss upon it, and made it His friend: *quoniam voluisti me*. What is the cold philosophical humility of those who recognise their littleness before the greatness of the Cosmos—after all, simply a difference of quantity—when compared with the glowing humility of the lover?

Opinions may legitimately differ as to how far the humility of the saint is a purely natural phenomenon. It is perhaps because so many of the characteristics of sanctity are not necessarily supernatural that the definitely miraculous element is so pronounced in the lives of most saints, for a miracle is God's way of marking out His saints from other men.

And this brings me to the difficulty that confronts a Catholic who hopes that his book may be read not only by those of the Faith but also by non-Catholics, a difficulty that may be illustrated from science.

Seven years after Dr. Mesmer effected his first hypnotic cures, scientists were still hysterically refusing even to appoint a committee to examine this new force. Indeed, nearly half a century was to pass before a special commission was appointed for the investigation of hypnotism. In those early days, a writer anxious to establish the reality of hypnotism would naturally have relied on the most evidential cases. He would have ignored cases that, though completely convincing to those who knew that hypnotism was a fact, would not be sufficiently convincing to overcome the resistance of reactionary skepticism.

Miracles today are in much the same position as hypnotism at the end of the eighteenth century. Few, if any, of those who have made a really scientific and persistent attempt to sift the evidence, at Lourdes and elsewhere, have remained completely skeptical. In arguing with a skeptic, we must naturally confine ourselves to miracles for which the evidence is coercive.

Once, however, we have established to our own satisfaction the fact that miracles occur beyond all possibility of doubt, we need not require, excepting for controversial purposes, much more evidence for any particular miracle than for any particular case of hypnotism.

Some of Fr. Claver's miracles are supported by no evidence worthy of the name; others are very fully attested. Some of these miracles belong to the category of phenomena that are accepted today, but which were once stoutly denied. Most scientists today accept the reality of telepathy. Many of my readers would certainly not question certain stories about Claver that our enlightened grandfathers would have rejected with scorn as characteristic examples of popish superstition. Case after case is recorded of his uncanny power of reading the minds of men. Uncanny and often embarrassing, for he knew exactly which sins the penitent preferred not to mention in the confessional. Again and again, Fr. Claver appeared on the scene, as though by a miracle, at some moment when a man was intending to commit suicide. It was a kind of uncanny second sight. On one occasion, he advised a colony where he was giving a mission to leave their homes, warning them that a troop of Englishmen would arrive and ravage the whole country. No news of a marauding English ship had reached South America, and yet this prophecy, which was received with complete surprise, was verified that night. The pirates landed and pillaged the district.

On another occasion, Fr. Claver suddenly left the house in which he was staying and made his way through the darkness and over the mountains until he discovered three poor slaves who had been abandoned in a miserable shed. Many other such incidents of telepathic power are recorded by his biographers.

His biography also contains familiar stories of exorcism, which the modern scientist might be inclined to pass if we allow him to relabel "possession" "dual personality."

A Saint in the Slave Trade

Fr. Claver's head was often seen surrounded by a halo of radiant light, yet another of these phenomena that would have been
dismissed unexamined by Huxley, but which have recently been
observed under rigid test conditions and which will, no doubt,
soon be provided with a nice, tidy, scientific label.

In the recent case of the "luminous woman" of Pirano is
an example, rich in humor, of the manner in which modern
science is being forced to recognize the reality of phenomena
whose existence is so distressing to the diehards of materialism.
Cinematograph records have been obtained of these luminous
appearances, and with the aid of the film thus provided, Dr.
Protti has submitted a provisional report to a medical society
connected with the University of Padua. Dr. Protti has convinced himself that the lady in question "has a fixed idea of a
religious character." This is scientific jargonese for "is a saintly
woman." And he also holds that "these fixed ideas can in particular subjects produce profound changes in the vegetative life
system." This is most reassuring. The day may be approaching
more rapidly than we expect when scientists will accept the
Resurrection as a rather striking instance of a profound change
in the vegetative life system of a body that has passed through
the process known as death.

All that the excellent Dr. Protti has done has been to establish, once again, the close association of supranormal phenomena
with intense religious conviction. No, that is not all, for he has
exposed the defective imagination of those superior people who
dismissed as grossly superstitious those witnesses in the past who
recorded precisely similar phenomena in connection with the
saints.

This book, however, is not a general discussion of miracles,
nor do I think that anything is to be gained by chronicling in

detail the many miracles performed by Fr. Claver.[18] Many of these miracles are as uninteresting to the Catholic as they are unconvincing to the skeptic. For, once one has accepted the fact that miracles occur, the actual record of miraculous cures is often as dull as a physician's notebook. But there is one miraculous story that may be told, if only for its charming sequel.

The story opens on conventional lines: a slave apparently dead, a remorseful master who remembers that he had put off until too late arrangements for the slave's Baptism. Fr. Claver, hastily summoned, kneels beside the slave, who gives no sign of life, and calls on her by name. The slave opens her eyes. "Please give a sign if you wish to be baptized."

"With all my heart," replies the slave.

Fr. Claver sends for water, administers the sacrament, and suddenly the slave rises and gives thanks to God for a complete cure.

The water that remained after the slave woman had been baptized was poured over a dying plant, perhaps in the half hope that the water in which the saint had dipped his hand for Baptism might retain some quickening grace. And the water worked the half-expected wonder, and the dying plant next day had burst into flower.

A symbol of Claver's influence over many withered souls in Cartagena.

---

[18] Professor Haldane and I have exchanged many letters on the subject of the miracles at Lourdes, letters published in *Science and the Supernatural*.

13

The Dying of Claver

Even before his final collapse, there were moments when the flesh scored one round at least in this losing fight with the spirit, moments when nature exacted a penalty for Claver's reckless disregard of health. During one of the illnesses, an attendant gave a startled exclamation on seeing that the sick man still wore his hair shirt next to his skin. "Father," he asked, "how long is the poor ass to be kept in harness?"

"Till death" was the reply.

Till death. And it seemed in 1650 that the "poor ass" would not long remain in harness. Claver was in the thirty-sixth year of his ministry and approaching the seventieth year of his life when the plague that was ravaging South America approached Cartagena.

Claver had been conducting a missionary campaign in the plague-stricken districts. He had crossed the pathless hills in steaming heat and beneath torrential rain. He was recalled to Cartagena, and within a few days of his return, he had gone down with the plague.

Many of his younger and healthier colleagues died, but God was preparing a testing time for Claver more severe than any of his self-inflicted penances. There are few things harder to bear than a sudden translation from a life of heroic activity to a life of complete helpless dependence. Claver could no longer say Mass. He had to give up hearing confessions after fainting continuously in the confessional.

Then came the moment when there was nothing to be done but to lie and wait for the end, which would not come. These last long years, four years in all, were to prove a veritable tragedy of neglect. The African to whom he was entrusted repaid with insults and unimaginative cruelty the gigantic debt that he and his owed to the man who had justified by blood and tears his claim to be the slave of the Ethiopians.

Perhaps this supreme trial was the culminating test of sanctity for which these long years of massive preparation had been designed. I have elsewhere quoted the tribute of the Jesuit who had known Fr. Claver in his novitiate and who was to meet him again in his declining years. The humility that had been so conspicuous in Claver the novice remained with him to the end, for Claver, as his friends said, was a novice to the last. Indeed, his long novitiate ended only with death.

So long as it was humanly possible for him to be moved, he had insisted on being carried at intervals to the harbor or to the hospitals. On his last visit to his beloved lepers, a horse was sent from the lazaretto to fetch the old saint, who was carried from his bed and firmly strapped onto the bewildered horse with the not surprising result that the horse bolted. Maddened by the flapping of Claver's famous cloak and the shouts of the crowd, the horse galloped wildly down the street. At last it came to a sudden stop. Kindly folk crowded round, unstrapped the old man, and lifted him tenderly to the ground. He seemed puzzled by their solicitude, for he had hardly noticed the peril in which he had been placed and had begun a prayer when they strapped him onto the horse, and the prayer was uninterrupted by its frenzied movements.

After this, perhaps his last emergence from the sickroom, an immense solitude formed itself round him. The college staff, which had been grievously thinned by the plague, was still appallingly overworked. The men who staggered home at night after a long day among the sick were only too ready to tumble exhausted into their beds.

The Jesuits knew that a slave had been appointed to look after Fr. Claver, and no doubt expected that the slave would report if there was anything wrong, and were perhaps glad to remember that the old man loved nothing better than to be left alone.

The devil should not be represented with horns and tail, but with a barrister's wig, for no counsel could be more skilled in throwing dust into the eyes of a jury than the devil when engaged in the plausible reinforcement of those dissuasions with which duty has always to contend. One can imagine an exhausted Jesuit collapsing into his bed after a day among the plague-stricken sick. Duty whispers that he has not seen Claver for weeks, and that it might be rather nice to look him up. And then the devil comes along with the silky voice of the special pleader: "Oh, well, Fr. Claver loves to be left alone. He props a big stone up against his door to have full warning if anyone intrudes on his prayers or his penances.... You say that this was before he fell ill.... Perhaps.... But even if he is neglected, the man has a love for suffering, and it would be a real shame to deprive him of this additional mortification, a very succulent morsel, believe me.... And anyhow, there are plenty of others.... And some of them may be visiting him at this moment.... It is the job of the Father Rector or the minister or the lay brothers.... Anyhow, you've had a terribly exhausting day."

Yes, one sees how it happened.

Meanwhile, there was Joachim, as the slave was called, crude, uncouth, unimaginative, fundamentally stupid rather than evil. Joachim becomes more and more contemptuous of the silent, helpless old man, whose absurd patience under reproach was itself a kind of divine reproof, all the more effective because unconscious. "There are," as Fr. Martindale observes, "few things so exasperating as to have a man patient at one's expense; silence may be the worst of snubs; and holiness, when it does not convert, may very easily drive the perverse into active evil."

An unpleasant fellow, this Joachim. If there was anything tasty on the dishes sent up from the kitchen, he would flick it off the plate with deft but dirty fingers. Claver was so helpless that he could not feed himself, and he may well have shrunk from the unattractive lumps of food that were conveyed to his trembling mouth by the unwashed fingers of this bullying slave. And there were days when Joachim simply did not come at all, and Claver lay, very still and uncomplaining, without food and without help. Sometimes he staggered to his feet in the hope of reaching the tribune from which he could hear Mass. Then the sacristan appeared, for the sacristy was immediately underneath Claver's bedroom, and asked him what had happened. Claver apologized humbly and never made the least complaint about the absentee, Joachim. He insisted, firmly but gently, that he would greatly regret a change, since he and Joachim were used to each other's ways.

Indeed, Fr. Claver may have felt grateful to Joachim for thus linking the closing scenes of his own martyrdom with memories of the Via Dolorosa. "And the soldiers also mocked him"(Luke 23:36), just like Joachim. And yet that tormented figure on the Cross was dying for the men who railed at Him. Why, then, should

His disciple in Cartagena complain just because one of those for whom he had toiled without resting repaid the debt in the hard coin of insult and neglect? "He was oppressed, and he was afflicted, yet he opened not his mouth" (Isa. 53:7). Yes, he and Joachim understood each other. It would be a pity if Joachim were dismissed.

Slave of the slaves, and at last God had taken him at his word. For in all these long years of his ministry, he had slaved for but had not been the slave of the Ethiopian. He was born free, and try as he might, he could not divest himself of the prestige of his race. He was white, and they were black. He might toil for them, he might suffer for them, but the sacrifice that he offered was a voluntary sacrifice, and there is a world of difference between the voluntary consecration of one's labor and of one's time and that complete subjection of which slavery consists. He had given to the blacks all that he could possibly give, but though he had suffered for them, he had not suffered from them. Now, at last, the roles were reversed. God had answered his prayer. In his own person, he was helping to pay the debt, the debt that had been incurred by the brutal slave traders. He paid it by suffering the noisome remnants of decaying food that Joachim had been too idle to remove, the plague of mosquitoes that buzzed round his bed and infected the dirt that was Joachim's legacy, and Joachim himself, strutting round the room with an insolence that would have been excessive had Claver been the slave and he the slave master.

Aethiopum semper servus. Praise be to God, he had at last paid for the title that he had himself selected when he had been raised to the peerage of the slaves.

Nor was this his only consolation. For there was one, at least, who did not leave Fr. Claver to Joachim and solitude. The eyes of the dying saint never left the one possession that he had retained throughout all these years: the picture that hung facing his bed, of Br. Alonso Rodriguez, the old gatekeeper who had sent him to Cartagena.

And, as the months passed, even Joachim seemed less crudely solid, as the veil between Claver and his old friend gradually became more transparent.

Meanwhile, Fr. Claver's successor had arrived, Fr. Diego de Farina. Claver heard the news with joy. At last he could die in peace, happy in the knowledge that he was not leaving his post unfilled. Summoning his last resources of strength, he somehow contrived to drag himself into Fr. Diego's room and to kiss the feet of the man who was to carry on his work.

And now the end was near. It was the midsummer of 1654, in the seventy-first or, as some believe, in the seventy-third year of his life and in the fifty-fifth of his entry into the Society of Jesus.

Fr. Claver was very happy, for he knew that his end had been ordained on the day when he would himself have chosen to die, the Nativity of Our Lady.

The government had ordered the demolition of that part of the college in which his own cell was situated. Had he not been dying, he might have welcomed this news with enthusiasm as a most attractive mortification.

But the dying saint knew that his work was done and that God would spare him the suffering that could no longer serve any purpose in his ministry. So when it was reported to him — it was then Saturday — that the demolition would begin on Monday, he replied serenely that God would spare him this grief and would allow him to die undisturbed in the cell in which he had lived for so long.

On Sunday, he was allowed to hear Mass, supported by two slaves. On Monday, the hammers of the workmen could be heard along the passage. The walls were collapsing beneath their blows. Claver smiled. He knew that he would have left his little cell before those dear walls that had encompassed him for so long began to fall.

Suddenly the rumor of his approaching end ran through the sweltering streets of Cartagena, and the memory of his long ministry crystallized into a wave of passionate grief. The door of the college was besieged by a tempestuous mob of nobles, priests, and common people. The Jesuits had locked the gates, but wave after wave broke against them until at last they burst open. Then came another wave: the slaves who had heard that their apostle was dying—the slaves freed for once from the restraining fear of their betters—they, too, poured into the little cell and prostrated themselves at the feet of their beloved missionary. And perhaps by this time, even Joachim had found his way to his knees.

And then came a flood of little children, and they too refused to be denied.

And around his bed men fought desperately for relics. There was little to fight for, but the poverty of the cell was gleaned by avaricious hands. Only the picture of Br. Alonso remained, stubbornly defended by a Jesuit, who had to use his fists to spare Fr. Claver so grievous a deprivation.

And perhaps that picture was the one thing in the room of which Fr. Claver was still conscious. Very shadowy were the forms that poured in and out of his cell, very faint the angry voices in the passage from those who clamored to enter, and the still angrier voices of the Jesuits whose frayed nerves were giving under the strain of controlling the surging mob. The "muddy vesture of decay" was wearing very thin.

And the solitude of years once again took possession of the cell in which men were fighting for elbow room.

A Saint in the Slave Trade

The end came between one and two o'clock on the morning of Tuesday, September 8, the feast of Our Lady's Nativity. It was her birthday ... and his. Suddenly the solitude of his cell was filled with voices. The wilderness and the solitary place were glad and the desert rejoiced and blossomed like a rose. And the picture on the wall came to life, and Fr. Claver stretched out his arms to meet the embrace of the old gatekeeper who had first set his feet on the road that led to the Caribbean Sea and to the happiness that God hath prepared for them that love Him.

Part 2

Supplementary Questions

14

The Conquest of Happiness

Among the many things for which I am indebted to my friend J. B. S. Haldane is a more intimate knowledge than I should otherwise possess of the waiting rooms at Petts Wood and Orpington, for I find it difficult not to be carried beyond Chislehurst on the days when his controversial letters arrive; and it is to Haldane that I owe my introduction to Mr. Snooter of the well-known city firm Snooter, Simpkins, and Snooter. It happened like this. I was so engrossed in Haldane's thesis that no really nice deity could have made parasite worms that I had to jump from a moving train onto Chislehurst platform. In the excitement of the moment, I left behind the *Universe* and removed the *Financial Times* belonging to Mr. Snooter. Chance decreed that I should find myself next day in the same carriage as Mr. Snooter, who lives at Orpington. He took down his dispatch case from the rack and produced the *Universe*.

"I always return lost property when I can," he said rather stiffly. He made me feel most uncomfortable.

"I am afraid," I confessed, "that I cannot return the compliment, but I only hope that you found the *Universe* as interesting as I found the *Financial Times*. I think there is something to be said, don't you, for these enforced introductions to new periodicals. I was so interested to discover from the *Financial Times* that there was no demand for money in the city, a fact that has revolutionized my conception of city men, and that apparently a contango is not, as I always imagined, a queer kind of animal domiciled in the antipodes. I do hope that you, too, picked up a few scraps of useful information from a paper that, I imagine, you do not normally read."

"Well, I did have a look at it," he said, "but I can't say that that sort of thing is much in my line."

He paused, and I could see from his expression that he was turning over in his mind a thought, the kind of thought that Catholics are forbidden by their priests to think. My instinct was right. He began to explain that he was not a churchgoer because he worshipped God under the blue dome of Heaven — his car, I suppose, must have a sunshine roof. And like other blue-domists, he could not understand why anybody should ever worship God in a stuffy church. But, of course, Catholics had to go to church, hadn't they?

This thought carried us to Hither Green, and the much-of-a-muchness of all religions brought us to Lewisham. New Cross and St. John's served to punctuate the paragraph in which he contrasted the importance of helping lame dogs over stiles with the unimportance of dogma and incense and all this fuss about candles.

"There was an article in that paper," he continued, "about saints, and how they love suffering. What I say is this. It doesn't matter what religion a man belongs to. Happiness is the test, being happy oneself and helping to make other people happy. But what good does all this hair shirt business do? Does wearing a hair shirt make a man happy? Does it help to make other people happy? That's what I want to know."

Of course happiness is the test, but the world is not divided into fanatics who prefer unhappiness to happiness, average Christians who don't mind one way or the other, and sensible Snooters who very definitely prefer happiness to misery. It is not as simple as all that.

It would be more plausible to divide people into those who feverishly pursue pleasure without achieving happiness and saints who have discovered that suffering is a triumph that purchases a happiness unobtainable by self-indulgence—plausible, but misleading, for no true saint is capable of such cold-blooded calculation. The saint is not a prudent investor but an ardent lover, and the extravagances of his devotion cannot be measured in terms of profit and loss.

I should find it easier to discuss hair shirts with my friend if I could only persuade him that there are more ways than one of approaching this problem. We can start from the Christian premise that the next world is more important than this or from the humanist premise that the grave ends all. Now, a Christian and a humanist can pass the time pleasantly between Chislehurst and Charing Cross in discussing which premise is correct, but it is tiresome to discuss hair shirts with a man who unconsciously assumes, as so many people assume today, that the Christian has, for form's sake, to profess a belief in the next world, but that he is really too sensible not to realize that it is this life that really matters. This little misunderstanding clouds most discussions between Christians and other people, for the humanist, instead of attacking the Christian premise, proves with great triumph that the Christian conclusions cannot be deduced from the humanist premise. Of course they cannot. If this life be all, it would be impossible to justify by reason the strange behavior of Peter Claver even though we might still feel that his folly was not ignoble.

A Saint in the Slave Trade

The Christian does not accept the humanist premise that the sole criterion of conduct is its effect on our comfort and happiness in this world, and consequently the humanist must either disprove the Christian premise or show that Christian conclusions do not follow consistently from that premise.

It is interesting to note that even if we accept, for the sake of argument, the humanist premise that happiness in this world is the only sane criterion of conduct, we should reach the paradoxical result that Christian conduct satisfies the criterion of the humanist and that humanist conduct does not. Happiness, in other words, evades the man who consciously pursues it, whereas experience confirms the paradox of Thomas à Kempis: "When you shall have got so far that tribulation is sweet to you and savours of Christ, then indeed it will be well with you, and you will have discovered Paradise on earth."[19]

Mr. Bertrand Russell has written a book called *The Conquest of Happiness*. His prescription is very different from that of Thomas à Kempis, but it remains to be seen whether the young people who share his contempt for religion will conquer with his assistance the happiness that they desire. At the moment, the prospects are none too hopeful. "It is notorious today," writes my late opponent Dr. Joad,

> that heavenly rewards no longer attract and infernal punishments no longer deter with their pristine force; young people are frankly derisive of both, and, seeing no prospect of divine compensation in the next world for the wine and kisses that morality bids them eschew in this one, take more or less unanimously to the wine and kisses. Unfortunately

---

[19] Thomas à Kempis, *The Imitation of Christ*, 2, 12, 11.

the pleasurable results anticipated from these sources fail to materialize. That unchecked indulgence in the more obvious types of pleasure is unsatisfying is the unanimous teaching of those who have had the leisure and opportunity to try them in all ages. It is the more unfortunate that it is a truth which nobody believes to be true until he has discovered it for himself.... You cannot take the kingdom of pleasure, any more than you can take the kingdom of beauty, by storm.[20]

And he adds, "For the first time in history there is coming to maturity a generation of men and women who have no religion, and feel no need for one. They are content to ignore it. Also they are very unhappy, and the suicide rate is abnormally high."[21]

The new recipes for happiness are not giving complete satisfaction. Young people of today no longer quote with hearty defiance a famous line from Swinburne that the youthful rebels of the eighties hurled at their Victorian fathers.

> Thou has conquered, O pale Galilean,
> And the world has grown grey with thy breath.

For the advent of the pale secularist has not, as yet, ushered in an age of uproarious fun.

Which is disappointing.

Perhaps there is something to be said for a reasoned examination of the older recipes. It may conceivably be true, as St. Peter Claver believed, that happiness does not depend on the

---

[20] Cyril Edwin Mitchinson Joad, *The Present and Future of Religion* (London: E. Benn, 1930), 82–83.

[21] Ibid., 91.

environment but on the mind. It is difficult to avoid an uncomfortable suspicion that the humanitarianism that devotes all its energies to raising the standard of comfort sometimes lowers the standard of happiness by rendering men less capable of bearing such evils as they cannot escape. As Tyrrell says, "Instead of inuring men to the rough climate of this mortal life, humanitarianism has accustomed them to wraps and mufflers, and rendered them susceptible to every little change of temperature—poor, frail, pain-dreading creatures."

Popular atheism is often unconsciously inspired by an illogical hatred of the deity whose very existence atheists profess to deny. It is impossible to work oneself up into a state of rage against something that does not exist, and the moral indignation that is the driving force behind such atheism as still exists is inspired much less by academic doubt of God's existence than by the fact that God permits pain and suffering. If pain tended to disappear as religion declines, the Church would have to fight for its existence, but the history of Russia since Russia officially adopted atheism as the state philosophy lends no support to this view.

There is nothing in Christianity that forbids and much in Christianity that encourages all men of goodwill to prosecute with the utmost vigor the struggle against disease and suffering. And as there is no reason to suppose that cancer and cathedrals would vanish simultaneously, there is surely something to be said for a religion that teaches men not only to relieve the sufferings of others but also to accept with courage and—supreme paradox—with gratitude the inescapable sufferings that come their way.

15

The Conquest of Pain

The humanist has more excuse for equating pain and evil than for confusing happiness with pleasure. For one need not be a Christian to admit the inescapable fact that happiness may enter by the gate through which pleasure departs—the gate of suffering. Many a Roman was converted to Christianity by the radiant happiness on the faces of young girls as they entered the arena. And it may well have been the Christian martyrs whom Seneca records as enduring the most frightful torments "without a groan, nay, more, they asked for no remission; and more, not a word could be extorted from them, yet more they laughed and this right heartily."

Happiness, then, must not be confused with pleasure. Pleasure is a stranger to the torture chamber, but happiness has sometimes defied even the rack.

All of which is no discovery of Christianity. "That pain and happiness, in their natures opposite, are yet linked together in a kind of necessary connection" was a fact that Livy had observed. The sentence is aptly quoted by Whymper on the title page of *Scrambles Amongst the Alps.*

"How singular is the thing called pleasure," exclaimed Socrates, "and how curiously related to pain, which might be thought to be the opposite of it; for they are never present to a man at the same instant, and yet he who pursues either is generally compelled to take the other: their bodies are two and they are joined by a necessary single head."

The famous saying of Mohammed "Hell is veiled with delights, and Heaven in hardships and misery" finds an echo in all great philosophies, Christian and non-Christian.

Indeed, the very word *ascetic* comes to us from the pagan world and once meant no more than "exercise." To the Greek, the athlete was the typical ascetic, for he exercised his body by sacrificing the pleasures of self-indulgence to the happiness of self-discipline. He was, as St. Paul said, temperate in all things to win a corruptible crown. No illustration, as St. Paul knew, was more calculated to impress his hearers with the reasonableness of Christian asceticism, for where religion is weak, the ascetic instinct finds expression in the more strenuous sports.

It has been left to the modern world to discover that pain is not only the greatest of evils but also the most formidable argument against the existence of God. "A strange moral transformation," writes William James,

> has within the past century swept over our Western world. We no longer think that we are called on to face physical pain with equanimity.... The way in which our ancestors looked upon pain as an eternal ingredient of the world's order, and both caused and suffered it as a matter-of-course portion of their day's work, fills us with amazement....
>
> Where to seek the easy and pleasant seems instinctive—and instinctive it appears to be in man—any deliberate tendency to pursue the hard and painful as such and for their own sakes might well strike one as purely

abnormal. Nevertheless, in moderate degrees it is natural and even usual to human nature to court the arduous. It is only the extreme manifestations of the tendency that can be regarded as a paradox.[22]

This passage was written before the Wars, and the modern world was not as degenerate as William James feared. But war was followed by the inevitable reaction, and the "pain-dreading temper" that William James condemned has reasserted itself.

And this must be my excuse for restating an old truism, for it is necessary to remind ourselves from time to time that pain and evil are not necessarily synonymous, and that pain is a price that may cheerfully be paid for the nobler forms of happiness. To this truth, indeed, not only the Christian ascetic but the explorer and the mountaineer bear witness, and it is difficult to see why the Christian should be regarded as a paradoxical fellow for insisting on a truth that is part and parcel of the unchanging substance of human history. And not of human history alone. Pain would seem to be the price that has been paid for every advance from inorganic matter to man. Pain is almost unknown in the lower forms of life. A friend of mine once watched a crab who was contentedly feeding on a small crab while his own extremities were providing a larger crab with breakfast.

"The popular idea of the struggle for existence entailing misery and pain on the animal world," declared the great scientist Wallace,

> is the very reverse of the truth.... What it really brings about is the maximum of life and the enjoyment of life

[22] William James, *The Varieties of Religious Experience: A Study in Human Nature* (New York: Longmans, Green, 1917), 292–293.

with the minimum of suffering and pain. Given the necessity of death and reproduction—and without these there could have been no progressive development of the animal world—and it is difficult even to imagine a system under which a greater balance of happiness could have been secured.... The probability is that there is as great a gap between man and the lower animals in sensitiveness to pain as there is in their intellectual and moral faculties.

A fish is less sensitive to pain than a dog but probably gets far less fun out of life. The higher we climb in the scale of life, the greater the price paid in pain for a wider range of emotion and happiness. It is indeed possible, as Mr. Alfred Noyes suggests, that in a profoundly interdependent scheme, facts such as these may represent "some absolute necessity which even omnipotence could not overcome without self-contradiction. Is it not possible that if the highest aim of that scheme were ever to be realised, a price had to be paid, of which the perfect example was lifted up on the Cross whose arms point in opposite directions?"[23]

Even William James, disedified though he was by that extravagant love of pain that is the characteristic of Catholic sanctity, was candid enough to admit that "the folly of the Cross, though inexplicable by the intellect, has yet its indestructible, vital meaning."[24] Calvary, indeed, alone gives us the clue to facts against which atheists are in angry rebellion, facts for which atheism, however, is no remedy and no explanation.

---

[23] Alfred Noyes, *The Unknown God* (New York: Sheed and Ward, 1934), 271.
[24] James, *The Varieties of Religious Experience*, 356.

To the atheist, suffering is unintelligible; to the Christian, it is part of a scheme in which the sufferer is privileged to share in the divine act of atonement. Christianity, indeed, alone finds a rational place for suffering in its philosophy. "All the religious philosophies of antiquity," writes Dean Inge,

> shrink, in the last resort, from grasping the nettle of suffering quite firmly. They all want to make us invulnerable, somehow. There must always be a back-door of escape if the ills of life become too overpowering. Either defiant resistance, or suicide, or complete detachment, is recommended. By some means or other, the man himself must be rescued from circumstance; he must provide himself with a magic impenetrable armour. And *therefore* the sting of pain is never drawn. The good news of Christianity is that suffering is in itself divine. It is not foreign to the experience of God Himself. "In all their affliction he was afflicted." "Surely he hath borne our griefs and carried our sorrows." "If thou be the Son of God," said His enemies, "come down from the Cross." No: not while any man remains unredeemed. The divine suffering is not an episode, but a revelation. It is the necessary form which divine love takes, when it is brought into contact with evil. To overcome evil with good, means to suffer unjustly and willingly.
>
> It is the blasphemy of "Christian Science" and kindred movements to deny the Cross. And in our soft, self-indulgent age it is, shamefully, felt to be a greater difficulty in the way of belief in God that men should suffer than that men should sin. This timid, pain-dreading temper is thoroughly unchristian.

A Saint in the Slave Trade

I have just been rereading the letter from which I have already quoted in the preface, a letter written to Fr. Knox some time before I became a Catholic. "One cannot imagine Christ wearing a shirt stuffed with jagged nails, or flogging Himself till the blood ran. He died on the cross without a murmur, but He did not inflict torture on Himself. He did not go out of His way to make Himself uncomfortable, but He was completely indifferent to His comfort—a very different matter."

"He did not go out of His way to make Himself uncomfortable." Well, the God who became man may, in some sense, have been said to have gone out of His way, and a cross is certainly more uncomfortable than a hair shirt; and Christ who of His own free will embraced that supreme instrument of torture, certainly provided a precedent for the voluntary and self-inflicted suffering of the saints. For the Christ whom we worship is not a martyr nailed to an inescapable cross, but a God who chose Calvary and who could at any moment have descended from the Cross of His own choosing. If suffering is not foreign even to the experience of God Himself, if God by His own free choice shares in our pain, is it really so very difficult to understand why Peter Claver should have acted as if he really believed that suffering was divine? Is it really so strange that he should have slept every night on a bare floor, that he should have risen again and again from the floor to scourge himself until he bled, that a rough hair shirt was the only dressing that he applied to these self-inflicted wounds, that he should have worn near his body a rough wooden cross studded with points? For years no part of his body was free from pain either by day or by night. Must we dismiss all this as a painful and morbid aberration?

There is yet another possibility. The Christian, at least, cannot lightly dismiss the belief that there are souls who are specially

called to share in the work of Calvary, saints whose special vocation it is to offer up a life of heroic mortification as their contribution to the work of atonement for the sins of the world. Perhaps
this is the meaning of St. Paul's statement that he rejoiced in his
sufferings and filled up "that which is behind of the afflictions of
Christ" (Col. 1:24).

Those for whom this explanation of self-inflicted suffering is
too fantastic to deserve serious consideration may yet think less
hardly of these austerities when it is remembered that they in no
way weakened Fr. Claver's powers for good or militated against
his philanthropic activities. Nobody would have guessed that he
was never free from pain, for he responded to all appeals for help
with the alertness of an athlete reacting to the starter's pistol.
Indeed, his younger colleagues, as we have seen, complained
bitterly that he did not know the meaning of fatigue.

Certainly, Fr. Claver's austerities, judged wholly by the standard of practical philanthropy, had at least one great advantage.
He never suffered from that natural sense of inferiority that so
often, and so deservedly, handicaps the prosperous when called
upon to console the poor and the afflicted. He could meet on
equal terms the poor wretches who had been bruised by the
iniquities of the slave trade.

The most effective apostle is always the man who, like his
Master, is "acquainted with grief" (Isa. 53:3). Self-indulgent
preachers have sometimes secured ephemeral triumphs, for pulpit eloquence will carry a man very far, but it will not carry
him half so far as the inarticulate arguments of asceticism. The
imprint of the Cross is the only passport to the brotherhood of
the unfortunate.

During the writing of this chapter, I have been haunted by
an uneasy suspicion that the chapter itself is a confession of

failure, an admission that my retelling of Claver's life has been completely ineffective. For the reader who sees Claver as I see him may well be impatient of any attempt to justify this detail or that. Claver's life is the supreme argument for Claver's methods, and that life must be judged as a whole. It is, of course, possible for the humanist to praise Claver for feeding, washing, and consoling the slaves, to recognize the heroism of his work among the lepers, and, at the same time, to regard as an amiable weakness his efforts to convert the slaves to Christianity, and to dismiss with angry contempt, as a pathological aberration, his self-inflicted austerities. But a man would have to be obtuse not to suspect that there might be some casual connection between those elements of his life that are most offensive to the humanist and those achievements that so infinitely transcend in dynamic philanthropy the efforts of purely secular reformers.

16

The Flight from Pity

A recent survey of knowledge for young people in which the existence of God was denied, and in which Mohammed was and Christ was not thought worthy of mention, was defended by the publisher as a manifesto for the Sermon on the Mount, and by its editress as a magnificent exposition of practical Christianity. Had this lady been asked to define "practical Christianity," she would almost certainly have replied by quoting the second of the two great commandments: "Thou shalt love thy neighbor as thyself." But neighbor-loving, though a part, is not the whole of Christianity. This, indeed, would seem to have been Christ's view. But then, of course, Christ may not have been a practical Christian. Nothing, in the opinion of the modern world, could be less practical than the first great commandment: "Thou shalt love the Lord thy God with thy whole heart, and with thy whole soul, and with thy whole mind, and with thy whole strength."

Both commandments are difficult. It is much easier to believe in God than to love Him, and it is far less easy to love our neighbor than to devise schemes for his improvement. "Practical Christianity," in practice, too often means the denial of the first commandment, and the translation of the second commandment into a five-year plan for the regimentation of our neighbors.

A Saint in the Slave Trade

When I hear people talking glibly about practical Christianity and neighbor-loving, I am always reminded of the Modernist clergyman in *Fr. Malachy's Miracle*.

"I am afraid, sir," said Fr. Malachy, "that you are not a Christian."

"Not as you interpret the word, perhaps," replied the Rev. Humphrey Hamilton. "But if by being a Christian is meant serving others and not self, then I think I may humbly claim that distinction."

"I have always noticed," said Fr. Malachy, "that heretics and unbelievers are the first to take credit for observing a commandment so difficult that even the saints of God boggled over it."

Much of what passes for philanthropy in the modern world is not philanthropy in the exact sense of the term, for these alleged philanthropic activities are often inspired not by "love of man" but by ambition, self-importance, or that creative instinct that finds expression not only in art but also in organization and reconstruction.

"They analysed helpfulness recently," writes Fr. Ronald Knox, "in the psychological laboratory at Pharsalia, Ore. The analysis showed, I am told, the following results:

Love of interference	32 percent
Pride of workmanship	22 percent
Desire for gratitude	11 percent
Desire for admiration	11 percent
Self-importance	10 percent
Reaction from suppressed contempt	9 percent
Genuine moral altruism	5 percent"

Philanthropy, in the exact sense of the word—love of man—is seldom found excepting in a religious setting, for it is one thing to work for the benefit of humanity, as many secularists have done; it is quite another matter to love men. Indeed, there would seem to be some necessary connection between the first and the second great commandments, for the saints aflame with love of God have found it easier than other people to love their neighbors.

Much of what passes for pity in the modern world is not pity in the proper sense of the term, or rather it is pity as defined by the cynical Hobbes as "the imagining to oneself of a woe." It is an objection to being reminded of the existence of pain. The thought of suffering affects many people like a harsh color or the sound of a knife scraped along a stone wall.

Man is made in the image of God, and few men, whatever their creed, are completely pitiless. Yet the comparative absence of compassion was one of the most striking features of the pre-Christian world and is one of the consequences that always seem to follow the decline of Christianity.

Professor Mahaffy, in his book *Social Life in Greece from Homer to Menander*, has drawn a vivid contrast between the ideals of the Homeric chiefs and those of the medieval knights.

"We pass to the third element in chivalrous honour," he writes,

> a sense of *compassion* for the weak, and an obligation to assist the oppressed. Unfortunately this duty appears to have been delegated to Zeus, whose amours and other amusements often prevented him from attending to his business. How inadequately he performed it in this respect is plain from the very pathetic passages in which

the condition of the decrepit father, the forlorn widow, and the helpless orphan are described....

> No young companions own the orphan boy;
> With downcast eyes, and cheeks bedewed with tears,
> His father's friends approaching, pinched with want,
> He hangs upon the skirt of one, of one
> He plucks the cloak; perchance in pity some
> May at their tables let him sip the cup,
> Moisten his lips, but scarce his palate touch:
> While youths with both surviving parents blest
> May drive him from their feast with blows and
>   taunts:
> Begone, thy father sits not at our board!
> Then weeping to his widowed mother's arms
> He flies, that orphan boy, Astyanax.

It is here the lamentable condition of the orphan that strikes us so forcibly. How different, for example, do we find the Irish peasants, with whom I have already compared the Greeks, where the neighbours divide among them without complaint the children left destitute by the death or emigration of the parents, and extend their scanty fare and their wretched homestead to the orphan as to their own children. The Homeric gentleman, of whose refinement and delicate politeness we hear so much, was far removed from such generosity.[25]

It is interesting to compare Stoicism, not the least admirable aspect of the classical world, not only with modern

---

[25] John Pentland Mahaffy, *Social Life in Greece from Homer to Menander* (London: Macmillan, 1874), 29–30.

humanitarianism, which in some respects it so closely resembles, but also with the God-inspired philanthropy of the great saints.

The great Roman Stoics were groping after some theory of natural justice, but their humanitarianism was academic, cold, and sterile. We have seen that Christianity began by revolutionizing the status of the slave and finally brought about the disappearance of slavery. The process was slow, too slow, but the Christian leaven had worked from the first and ultimately permeated civilization with its influence. The Stoic apothegms in favor of liberty and natural law, though they were to influence the French and American revolutionists centuries later, had no influence whatever on the status of the contemporary slave.

Cassius, a famous Stoic, pleaded, for instance, with the Roman Senate for the rigid enforcement of the cruel law that decreed that if a slave murdered his master, every slave under that roof should be executed. Cassius was successful, and six hundred slaves were put to death because one of them had slain his master. Slaves who were past their work were often conveyed to an island in the Tiber and left to die of hunger.

Mr. Edwyn Bevan cites as evidence of that Roman attitude to slaves the following casual utterance of Horace's: "If you have a slave crucified because he takes a sly taste of the dish he is bringing you, you are justly thought to be abnormally ferocious. But if you cut a friend for some slight offence *how much worse* an action!"

No Stoic protested against the methods adopted for getting rid of unwanted children. Poor parents often placed their children at the foot of the Lactarian column, and rich mothers who were anxious for a male heir often discarded their superfluous daughters in the same place. Many of these children died; and the less fortunate were carried off by slave dealers. Pliny, a distinguished

Stoic, refers casually to the fact that the brains and marrow of these children were keenly sought after by superstitious persons. Seneca, who covered unending reams of paper with copybook maxims about virtue, praises on eugenic grounds the exposure of deformed children.

It is true that an occasional Stoic satisfied his conscience by an academic gesture of disapproval, but it needed the dynamic force of Christianity to transform academic humanitarianism into irresistible action. The Stoics, for instance, mildly disapproved of the amphitheater, but their disapproval was inspired not by any compassion for those who died to make a Roman holiday but by the belief that such scenes should not appeal to the cultured Stoic. What pleasure, asks Cicero, can a cultured man derive from seeing some poor wretch torn to pieces by wild beasts: *Sed quae potest homini esse polito delectatio?* Cicero, in other words, felt a cultured disdain for people who enjoyed these scenes of horror, but he felt no pity for the victim of the Games.

Cicero urged his politer readers to stop away from the Games; he did not urge them to stop the Games. And so the Games continued until a monk called Telemachus, who was certainly not a *homo politus*, was impolite enough to register a rude and vulgar protest by leaping into the arena himself. He sealed his protest with his blood, and from that moment, the Games ceased. The dynamic force of a humanitarianism inspired by the love of God succeeded where academic humanitarianism had failed.

Now, the force that impelled Telemachus into the arena was a new force. Compassion had no place in the Stoic scheme. Seneca summed up the attitude of the Stoic when he declared that we should show clemency but that we should try not to feel pity.

The Stoic's admiration for virtue was, in effect, self-admiration. He was interested not in the feelings of other people but in the development of his own admirable character. Plutarch, for instance, condemned anger not because an angry man was a nuisance to other people but because an angry man was a nuisance to himself. He confessed that he had been in the habit of punishing his slaves severely because, as is well known, slaves degenerate rapidly if they are not frequently beaten. "Later on," he wrote, "I realised that it was better to let the slaves deteriorate through my forbearance rather than to pervert myself by bitterness and anger for their reformation."

On one occasion, a slave whom Plutarch had ordered to be flogged taunted him with inconsistency and referred him to his own book on controlling anger. Plutarch replied that he was not in the least angry. "My face," he said, "is not flushed, there is no foam on my lips, why, I have not even raised my voice." Then Plutarch turned to the man who was flogging the slave and added, "While he and I are debating this point, do you carry on with your flogging."

The Roman Stoic fingering his pulse to prove that he was not in the least incensed while the slave was being flogged in his presence stands as a type of classical humanitarianism. Plutarch was in some respects an admirable man, but he was in love not with God but with Plutarch.

It was, perhaps, of such men that St. Augustine was thinking when he declared that "the virtue of the pagans is pride," seeing that their conduct was dictated not by the love of God but by the love of self.

The growth of pity, almost unknown in the classical world, is described by the atheists as the slow progress of civilization. It is a strange coincidence, however, that the reforms that the humanist credits to an abstraction called progress were first introduced in Christian lands and tardily adopted by such non-Christian countries as had come under the influence of Christian thought. It is surely significant that almost all those who have passed on the torch of protest against cruelty and oppression have claimed an apostolic succession derived from Christ. The reformers who rejected Christianity attacked abuses by appealing to Christians to practice the principles for which Christ died. For Christians, indeed, as I remarked in my controversy with Dr. Joad, have been alternately incited to reform by the appeal of saints and goaded into reform by the taunts of skeptics. Atheists, as we have seen, all unconsciously appeal to the Christian standard when they claim to be exponents of practical Christianity. What atheist ever professed to believe in "practical Mohammedanism"?

"Since Christ came into the world, there has no longer been a world without Christ: He entered into it like a dye, the stain of which no amount of washing will remove; like a drop of God's blood which remains ineffaceably there."[26]

And when Christ is forgotten, the flight from pity begins. The Renaissance was the rebirth not only of the Roman arch, but also of Roman pitilessness. The hospitals that had been built in honor of Christ began to decline when men celebrated the rebirth of Apollo. "When the pagan pomp of the Renaissance unfurled itself," writes Fr. Martindale, "care for human misery disappeared. When the beauty of the body was being worshipped, the very sight of sick or ugly bodies was abominated. The hospitals became plague spots of moral as well as of physical horror."

The hold of Christianity is always precarious, and where that hold is relaxed, the ancient brutality returns. Nowhere would you find a greater callousness toward individual suffering, or a greater lack of interest in misfits and social failures, than in the

---

[26] Wittig, quoted by Ida Coudenhove in *The Burden of Belief*.

one great European country that formally apostatized from the Christian faith.

Humanitarianism approaches the old standards of the Roman Stoics when it retreats from Christianity. If religion declines, we shall witness an increasing tendency to be interested in health statistics rather than in the sick, in averages rather than in individuals. The cult of efficiency will gradually oust the instinct of compassion.

A well-known doctor recently commented in my presence on the growing impatience in medical circles with incurables, for an incurable spoils hospital statistics. He believes that there is a growing demand for the painless extinction of incurable and bedridden paupers, a demand that is a logical deduction from the premise of atheistic humanitarianism.

Humanitarianism divorced from religion soon dissolves into an irrational sentimental worship of abstractions such as humanity. Of all forms of idolatry, humanity worship is perhaps the silliest; silly and yet pathetic, for there is pathos in the attempts of men to satisfy with husks their hunger for God.

Humanity worship is the theme of *Men in White*, which has played to full houses both in London and in New York. Dr. Braddock, one of the chief characters, consecrates his life to Humanity with a capital H. Nothing matters to Dr. Braddock but medical science, and, as his students know, he is the most exacting of taskmasters, for he expects from them the same sacrifices that he himself has made.

The keynote to the play is provided by a scene between Dr. Braddock and the young woman whom he has just persuaded to sacrifice her lover to her lover's profession. "You don't matter," says Dr. Braddock cheerfully to the lady. "I don't matter. Humanity alone matters"—a sentiment that does more credit to his heart than to his head. Humanity is a collection of "you's" and "I's." If you don't matter, and if I don't matter, humanity doesn't matter, for the sum of an infinite number of zeros equals zero.

And note that Braddock does not say, "You matter, but the part matters less than the whole, and therefore you matter less than humanity." He says, "You don't matter at all."

Christ commanded us to worship God and to love our neighbor as ourselves. Worship humanity, says the modern humanitarian, and hate yourself like your neighbors. Neither you nor he matters.

A Christian Braddock would not have needed to desert the firm ground of reason for an emotional appeal. He could have appealed to the Catholic doctrine of vocation in support of his belief that this brilliant young doctor should not retire from the hospital to a comfortable private practice in order to give more time to his wife, but continue for many years the exacting life of assistant to Dr. Braddock. "You matter frightfully," he should have said, "and your fiancée matters frightfully, but you both matter less than your vocation. You have a vocation for medicine, for the noble ministry of relieving pain, and to that vocation everything must be sacrificed. Fortunately your vocation does not involve vows of chastity, since you would find great difficulty in keeping such vows, but your vocation does demand great sacrifice. But your life will never be happy if, like the young man in the parable, you turn sorrowfully away. And remember that there is no unhappiness to compare with the unhappiness of those who sacrifice vocation on the altar of pleasure."

Dr. Braddock, in the play, is represented as a merciful and compassionate man, but then Braddock, like most humanitarians, is still impregnated by the ethic of Christianity. Obviously the worship of humanity must exclude compassion for the individual, for if humanity alone matters, we must be ready to sacrifice mis-fits to improve the general average. Pity, indeed, as our more consistent eugenists are the first to admit, is definitely dysgenic, a fact that Mr. H. G. Wells fully realizes.

"The world and its future," writes Mr. Wells, "is not for feeble folk any more than it is for selfish folk. It is not for the multitude but for the best. The best of today will be the commonplace of tomorrow. If I am something of a social leveller, it is not because I want to give silly people a good time, but because I want to make opportunity universal, and not miss out one single being who is worth while."

"Let the Lord God be praised in *all* His creatures," said St. Francis. For in the sight of God there is no single being who is not worthwhile.

The further men move from the Christian doctrine of the infinite value of every human soul, the more rapidly will they approach the Utopia of the humanist, in which the unfit and the incurables will be peacefully extinguished with all possible humanity by the most kindly of humanitarians.

And if there were no other world than this, there is a great deal to be said for eliminating from the contest those who have no chance of a prize. But if Christianity be true, the greatest of all prizes is within the reach of all. It is mainly chance that de-termines whether a man achieves intellectual, social, or athletic distinction, for brains, social status, and physique are accidents of birth. It is thus largely a matter of luck whether a particular individual becomes a Fellow of All Souls or a member of what was on one occasion most felicitously described as "the most enviable Order of the Victoria Cross." But it is the fact, not the accidents, of birth that qualifies a man for the most enviable of all orders, the Companionate of Heaven.

A Saint in the Slave Trade

Mr. Wells does not want to give silly people a good time, and if this world be all, Mr. Wells is right. If the grave ends all, there is no real reason why we should waste effort over the foolish and the unintelligent. I am not attacking Mr. Wells; on the contrary, I am grateful to him for stating so lucidly the conclusions that logically follow from the humanist premise. The humanitarianism that pretends to be concerned with the fate of "feeble folk" and "silly people" is, as Mr. Wells states by implication, a parasitic growth on the Christianity that it rejects. The humanitarianism that wishes to "make opportunity universal" and is prepared to sacrifice "silly people" on the altar of efficiency is alone consistent and logical. And for this reason, if for no other, "silly people" who are silly enough to believe that they have as much claim to a good time as Mr. Wells will be very silly indeed if they entrust their destinies to leaders who share Mr. Wells's views.

17

Catholic Humanism

"But now the time has come to go away. I go to die and you to live, but which is better is known only to God."

Not all of those who remember Socrates's last words to his judges realize why Socrates welcomed death.

During the last hours of his life, he explained to his friends that death was welcome because it freed his soul from the prison of the flesh. The true philosopher must be anxious to sever the soul from the communion of the body, for the soul cannot attain to truth so long as she is deceived by the body. The body "fills us full of love, and lusts, and fears, and fancies of all kinds, and endless foolery, and in fact takes away from us the power of thinking at all. But if we would have pure knowledge of anything, we must be quit of the body. The true philosophers have been in every way the enemies of the body, and desired to be alone with the soul."

Xenophon assures us that, had Socrates made the least effort to conciliate his judges, he would have been acquitted. The testimony of his friends and all the available evidence confirms the fact that Socrates had no real wish to live. He welcomed death because he despised the body, a fact that I commend to the attention of those ill-informed people who believe that Christianity taught men to distrust the body, which the Greeks worshipped.

A Saint in the Slave Trade

This contempt for the body, which is the very foundation of Platonic philosophy, represents a natural reaction from the gross licentiousness of the world in which Socrates and Plato lived.

Nobody, as Mr. Chesterton very rightly remarks, has ever written a real moral history of the Greeks.

> Nobody has seen the scale of the strangeness of the story. The wisest men in the world set out to be natural; and the most unnatural thing in the world was the very first thing they did. The immediate effect of saluting the sun and the sunny sanity of nature was a perversion spreading like a pestilence. The greatest and even the purest philosophers could not apparently avoid this low sort of lunacy. Why? It would seem simple enough for the people whose poets had conceived Helen of Troy, whose sculptors had carved the Venus of Milo, to remain healthy on the point. The truth is that people who worship health cannot remain healthy.[27]

Is it surprising that Plato, who lived in a society that idealized perversion, and that ascribed the grossest of carnal acts to the gods, should have despaired of the body? "The conception of sexual desire as essentially evil and unclean was not something which Christianity brought into the Graeco-Roman world," writes Dr. Edwyn Bevan in his admirable book on Christianity in *The Home University Library*, "but something which infiltrated into Christianity from that world. From the sixth century B.C., when the Orphics spread through the Greek world with their motto, 'the Body a tomb,' there has been this ascetic strain in Greek society.... It comes out markedly in Plato."

[27] G.K. Chesterton, *St. Francis of Assisi*, chap. 2.

It does indeed, and against the Platonic *dénigrement* of the body, the Incarnation was a splendid protest, for the body that Socrates despised was deemed worthy to become the tabernacle of God Himself.

"Deus, qui humanae substantiae dignitatem mirabiliter condidisti et mirabilius reformasti,... qui humanitatis nostrae fieri dignatus est particeps."

The Christ whom we praise "wonderfully dignified and still more wonderfully renewed the human nature of which He deigned to become partaker."

And now turn back to the *Phaedo*. "And thus, having got rid of the foolishness of the body, we shall be pure and hold converse with the pure."

What contrast could be greater?

Platonism, Stoicism, and their modern equivalents are eclectic philosophies, which may serve the needs of intellectual cliques, but which lack that warm humanity that we find in the Church, the natural home of the whole human race.

Christ did not despise the body, nor did He despise ordinary folk who, then as now, were so much more conscious of their bodies than of their souls. He mixed freely not only with saints but with sinners and gave scandal to the sour Puritans of the day because He "came eating and drinking" (Matt. 11:19). They contrasted Him unfavorably with St. John the Baptist. "Behold a man," exclaimed his enemies, "gluttonous, and a winebibber, a friend of publicans and sinners" (Matt. 11:19).

Christ would not have been a welcome guest at wedding feasts had His hosts felt uncomfortable every time a well-cooked dish appeared upon the table. His presence cast no shadow on the wedding feast, and laughter did not die down at His approach, for though there is a place in Christianity for the asceticism that forgoes, there is no place for the Puritanism that condemns in-nocent pleasure.

The attitude of the New England Puritan Alleyne as recorded in his diary, is, for instance, essentially anti-Christian. "On Wednesday, the 12th," he wrote, "I preached at a wedding and had the happiness thereby to be the means of excluding carnal mirth." Had Christ been a sour Puritan after Alleyne's pattern, He would not have turned water into wine; He would have ensured against "carnal mirth" by turning wine into lemonade.

The Christian view of sex is thus a mean between two ex-tremes, and it has not always been easy for Christians to maintain this balance of sanity. Christianity was born into a world that was ridden with sex, a world in which a Puritan reaction was overdue. It is not surprising that the "deep weariness and sated lust" of paganism should have produced in Christianity a reac-tion not dissimilar to that which it produced on Plato. Nor is it surprising that Christendom should have suffered intermittently from the Platonic infection, an infection that has taken many forms, for Gnosticism, Manicheism, and Puritanism are all akin to the Platonic heresy, and are all impregnated by distrust of the body, and by the conviction that pleasure is suspect.

Jung, who is no friend to Christianity, realized the nature of the problem with which the early Church was confronted.

The meaning of Christianity and Mithraism is clear. It is a moral restraint of animal impulses. The dynamic appear-ance of both religions betrays something of that enormous feeling of redemption which animated the first disciples and which we today scarcely know how to appreciate. Those old truths are empty to us. Most certainly we should still understand them had our customs even a breath of ancient brutality, for we can hardly realize in this day the whirlwinds of the unchained libido which roared through the ancient Rome of the Caesars.[28]

If ever, as is not inconceivable, the "unchained libido" should roar through the streets of our modern cities, the Church will reaffirm the ascetic ideal.

All of which helps us to understand the most famous example in history of a left-handed compliment; but St. Paul should be judged not by his grudging concession that it is better to marry than to burn but by his tremendous comparison between human marriage and the marriage of Christ to His Church. "So ought men to love their wives," he writes, "as their own bodies. He that loveth his wife loveth himself . . . and they two shall be one flesh. This is a great mystery: but I speak concerning Christ and the church" (Eph. 5:28–32).

"As humanity," writes Mr. Christopher Dawson in his summary of St. Paul's teaching, "is saved and deified by Christ, so the animal functions of sex and reproduction are spiritualized by the sacrament of marriage."

The Church, even when confronted with the "unchained libido" of the ancient world, never countenanced for one moment the heresy that sex is unclean. Indeed, the main object for which the medieval Inquisition was founded was to suppress the Cathari, a heretical sect whose principal tenet was the essential wickedness of all sexual intercourse, even in marriage.

In the centuries that followed, centuries during which the philosophy of the Faith was gradually developed by the great

[28] Carl Gustav Jung, *Psychology of the Unconscious*, trans. Beatrice M. Hinkle (New York: Moffat, Yard, and Company, 1916), 79–80.

Doctors of the Church, the balance of humanism in Christianity triumphed at every stage against the exponents of an exaggerated and merely negative asceticism. For Catholic asceticism, as we shall see, is positive rather than negative.

No theologian has asserted with greater conviction than St. Thomas the beauty of all created things. Nobody has banked with greater conviction on the fact that in the beginning God saw "every thing that he had made, and, behold, it was very good" (Gen. 1:31).

The humanism of St. Thomas is the theme of a thought-provoking essay, "On Being Human," by a modern Dominican. "Thomism"—that is to say, the theology of St. Thomas Aquinas—"regards the humanism of Greece," writes Fr. Vann, "not as mistaken, but as incomplete, for in each of these several values something is lacking; it regards the neo-pagan humanism of the Renaissance period as atrophied, for something is spurned. . . . St. Thomas did not mean to show merely that the Greek could at a pinch accommodate himself to Christianity, but on the contrary that Christianity was necessary to him, since it alone was capable of fully guaranteeing his ideal and allowing of its complete realization."

"The beauty of creatures," Fr. Vann continues, "is as vivid in the Thomist view as in the Hellenic, for while their beauty is infinitely inferior to the beauty of God, it is no less true, as St. Thomas tells us, that the beauty of creatures is nothing else than the likeness of God. . . . There is nothing which does not participate in beauty and goodness, since each thing is beautiful and good according to its proper form."

In his unqualified rejection of the Manichean heresy that visible beauty is a snare, St. Thomas, of course, is not alone. Full liberty, for instance, is defined by St. Teresa as that which "enables us to find God in all things and to use creatures as a means of raising ourselves to Him."

The created beauty of this world is not a rival to but a reflection of the uncreated beauty of God.

I do not think that St. Thomas would be disedified by the vigor with which the neo-Thomist Fr. Vann carries the war into the enemy's camp:

> Catholicism is positive, not negative. The religions which have come of a revolt from the Catholic position are by that fact largely negative; but the Catholic, on the contrary, is a man who is always affirming, and denying only in order to affirm. He denies himself only to affirm himself. His faith is positive, his dogma is positive, his morals are positive, his life is positive. An evolution, not a retrenchment. The Catholic does not believe that a negative denial of his personality as such can be pleasing to God. But he thinks restraint necessary for that greater fulfilment which is pleasing to his God. The negative is a mere means; it is the positive which is the end and purpose.

Christian humanism finds a place for asceticism in its scheme, for the man who abstains from, no less than for the man who drinks, wine. Indeed, asceticism is an integral part of the complete Christian life. But there is a fundamental difference between the positive asceticism of Christianity and the negative asceticism of Plato and the Platonists.

Christ came to teach us not to deny life but to complete it. He came that we might have life and have it more abundantly. The humanism of Christ is infinitely more complete, more complex, more varied, and richer than the humanism of Greece.

A Saint in the Slave Trade

I am prepared for the rejoinder that I began by criticizing Socrates for distrusting the body and by attempting to prove the superiority of that Christian humanism that includes the hair shirt and self-scourging.

It would indeed be difficult to justify what I have said if the strange behavior of Peter Claver is to be regarded as the norm to which all Christian behavior should approximate. But this is not the case. For a wholehearted admiration of St. Peter Claver is not irreconcilable with the conviction that the road that he followed is not the only road that leads to Heaven. There are many vocations, for God calls different men to different tasks, some to the life of the cloister, others to married life in the world. In other connections people are ready to admit that there is work that is best done by men with no outside responsibilities, work that is so absorbing that it demands a single-minded devotion that is possible only to the celibate. It is, for instance, possible to share Lord Kitchener's conviction that the army is all the family that a serious soldier needs, without regarding sex as unclean. Nor are those who assert that celibates make the best dons and the best schoolmasters usually accused of making a general attack upon matrimony.

The Church honors celibacy but also regards marriage as one of the sacraments of the Church. The widespread illusion that the Church regards matrimony as a grudging concession to fallen human nature is, perhaps, in the main due to a famous sentence in the Anglican marriage service: "Secondly, it was ordained as a remedy against sin, to avoid fornication, that such persons as have not the gift of continence might marry."

This sentence—incidentally, there is nothing in the least like it in the Catholic nuptial Mass—is responsible for a great deal of nonsense, of which the following is a fair sample:

"The church believed that men and women should love God, and that if they loved one another it interfered with that. So it was said by those in authority in the Church that it was sinful for men and women to be lovers, and celibacy (not marrying) was better than marriage. There was supposed to be something wrong about *sex* (being an adult, functioning, man or woman), and especially about being a woman; women were made to feel ashamed of themselves just because they were women." This paragraph is a quotation from a recent Outline of Knowledge intended for young people. It is a pity that the young man who wrote this hearty bosh had consulted neither the Catholic Missal nor the Anglican Prayer Book. He would have found in the former a prayer that contains this sentence: "O God, who hast consecrated the conjugal union by so excellent a mystery as to represent the sacrament of Christ and the Church by the mutual contract," and he would also find St. Paul's exhortation to husbands "to love their wives as their own bodies." Again, he would find that the Anglican marriage service opens in praise of matrimony as "an honourable estate instituted of God at the time of man's innocence, signifying unto us the mystical union that is between Christ and His Church; which holy estate Christ adorned and beautified with his presence by the first miracle that He wrought in Cana of Galilee."

Celibacy presents no difficulty to those who understand the Church's teaching on vocation, but there are other aspects of asceticism to which vocation is not a complete answer.

We must begin by clearly separating in our minds two things that the foolish and superficial habit of the moment habitually confuses: the Catholic asceticism, which is positive, and the Puritan, which is negative. In the beginning, God created all things and saw that they were good. It cannot be right to call bad that which God has called good.

A Saint in the Slave Trade

The Puritan commits the sin of blasphemy by condemning the beauty that comes from God. And even where he achieves the same end as the Catholic ascetic, he is actuated by a very different motive. His abstinence is inspired by distrust. He abstains from certain things because he believes those things to be bad. The Catholic ascetic, on the other hand, abstains from the same things precisely because he believes them to be good. If we wish to do honor to a friend, we give up something of our own that we value highly. We do not make him a present of something that we have saved for this purpose from the dustbin. The Catholic ascetic sacrifices his own pleasure but does not condemn the innocent pleasures of others. The Puritan takes pleasure in prohibiting the pleasures of other people. Many Catholics are teetotalers, for a Catholic is as free to abstain from wine as he is free to drink it, but no consistent Catholic could be a prohibitionist.

The great word *sacrifice* is in danger of losing its true meaning. "To understand what sacrifice means," writes Ida Coudenhove,

> we must go back to the pagans. For them it was a solemn and festal, a glad and beautiful affair; and only a valuable thing, indeed only the most valuable thing, was good enough to offer — the first-fruits of field and herd, the unblemished fruit, the choice, the rare, the precious.
>
> Even behind the darkest abuses, the sacrifice of children and kings, this conviction which we have so completely forgotten, is discernible. A sacrifice is a gift, chosen because it is precious; for the offering, it is anointed, crowned and garlanded, and the priest is clad in festal raiment, himself garlanded, incensed and greeted with songs. But what need to quote the pagans? Have you not noticed that the Church herself sacrifices with lights and

songs, amid flowers and incense? Or what is implied by that symbol of the Benedictine spirit, the never-ending liturgy of praise, but that the monks make their offering, the offering of their lives, as in a burst of song? How totally we have forgotten this! Sacrifice is giving—giving something to God.... But if this thing is vile and dangerous, how dare I offer to God what is, so to speak, too bad for me?

The saint is a friend of God, a phrase that, as Ida Coudenhove remarks, has been handed down by the agelong tradition of the Church. He is more than a friend; he is a lover in the heroic sense, a lover ever eager to prove his love by the extravagance of his gifts. And perhaps the self-inflicted austerities of the saint are due, as Fr. Vann suggests, to the longing of the lover to share in the sufferings of the beloved so that "nothing which the beloved has suffered may be strange and apart from the experience of the lover; for it is not a desire which is felt merely in regard to suffering which is here and now witnessed but of what is past and over as well."

"The saints," said Tyrrell, "were in love with God, and we are not," and therefore no extravagances of devotion will be demanded of us. Every Christian is called upon to aim at perfection, but he is not necessarily called upon to do certain extremely disagreeable things, such as taking vows of voluntary poverty or celibacy. Perfection consists in the submission of one's will to the will of God. We are all expected to be ready to surrender everything if God asks of us this surrender, but God does not ask this surrender of everybody. "Sell what thou hast, and give to the poor" was a command addressed not to the world in general, not even to all Christians, but to one particular individual. Nay, more, these words, strictly speaking, were not even a command to the young man who had great possessions. He had asked what he should do to merit eternal life, and Christ replied that he should keep the commandments. To which the young man smugly answered, "All these have I kept from my youth. What is yet wanting to me?" The time had come to put this very complacent young man in his place. "If thou wilt be perfect, go and sell what thou hast, and give to the poor" (see Matt. 19:21).

If thou wilt be perfect. Five words, but enough to reveal to the young man the vast gulf that separates holiness from good citizenship.

All of which seems to be leading by pleasant stages to a consoling conclusion that sanctity may well be left to the saint; in these, as in other matters, the amateur would be foolish to compete against the specialist along lines that the specialist has made peculiarly his own. Self-denial may be an extra, like carpentry in a preparatory school. The virtues that Christ practiced, like the profession that Christ followed, are not to be regarded as an integral part of the educational curriculum.

God does not expect the impossible. He will, we hope, make charitable allowances for those who have considerable difficulty in attaining a pass standard of virtue, but all Christians are expected to aim at an honors standard. The Church may perhaps be compared to a college that does not admit undergraduates who announce their intention of reading only for a pass degree but does not expel undergraduates who have little hope of anything better. "God," said Abraham Lincoln, "made so many ordinary people because He loves that kind of person." But ordinary people cease to be lovable when they develop a greasy self-satisfaction with their ordinariness. The publican was commended because he said, "God be merciful to me a sinner" (Luke 18:13). He did not ask for mercy because he was ordinary but because he was a sinner. At least he measured himself against the standard of piety, which the humanist rejects as irrelevant. The Catholic, in his approach to the humanist, is tempted to meet him on his own ground, and to accept, if only for the sake of argument, the humanist's standards. Piety is unfashionable.

It is, of course, legitimate to show that, even if we accept the standards of hedonism, Christianity is superior to hedonism, and Christian humanism richer than non-Christian humanism. Again, we are entitled to compare Catholic and non-Catholic culture, and to show even by the admission of those who reject Christianity that all great art derives its inspiration from religion. It is easy to make out a strong case for the Church as the patron of the arts, or as a cheery club pledged to wage war on ugliness and sour-faced Puritanism. All of which is true, but it is not the whole truth, nor even the most important truth, for the supreme concern of the Church is to produce not good artists and good fellows but good men.

We can make a temporary impression by commenting on those aspects of Catholicism that the intelligent humanist admires, and we can win his easy sympathy by proposing an alliance against all Puritans and killjoys. It is easy to bring a man to the point where he will admit that if he had any religion at all, he would be a Catholic, but we will make no lasting impression if we are secretly ashamed of the skeleton in the hair shirt.

We can, perhaps, break down prejudices by insisting on the glories of Catholic humanism, but we shall make no converts unless we emphasize the supernatural claims that are a stumbling block to the world. I remember as a boy listening to a school preacher singing the praises of a clergyman who had recently died, a clergyman who was recommended to us by the fact that he was "as good a cricketer as he was a Christian." He was particularly effective at cover point. You could not get a ball past him, and so on and so forth. I was not in the least impressed. I was surrounded by cricketers competing for my admiration, and I should have been much more interested in the deceased clergyman had the preacher proved that he possessed qualities that my youthful friends lacked. I should have been fascinated had he described a saint, for though I had met many good cover points, I had never met a saint.

It is tempting and, within reason, legitimate to meet the pagan on his own ground, but little more is achieved than a breaking down of prejudices.

St. Paul tried to meet the Greeks on their own ground when he preached at Athens. In his sermon on the Areopagus, he took as his text the inscription on the altar to the Unknown God, and tried to win the sympathies of his audience by allusions to Greek literature. "As certain also of your own poets have said ..." (Acts 17:28). It was perhaps of this sermon that he was thinking when he wrote his First Epistle to the Corinthians. "The Greeks," he said, "seek after wisdom: but we preach Christ crucified, ... unto the Greeks foolishness" (1 Cor. 1:22–23).

All of which has its lesson for us. We may attract the friendly attention of the modern Greeks by adapting St. Paul's sermon to modern needs: "As certain also of your own scientists have said ..." By such tactics we may break down prejudices; by such methods we may attract the wandering attention of those who today, as in St. Paul's time, "seek after wisdom"; by such an approach we may change the minds of men. But to change their hearts, the Church must preach Christ crucified, a foolishness to the Greeks of old and a scandal to the pain-dreading temper of the world in which we live.

18

Catholic Sanctity

The saint is the supreme argument for the reality of the supernatural, and it is significant that Dr. Inge, who rejects with contemptuous disgust the argument from miracles and who places little or no reliance on the historical accuracy of the Gospels, professes himself to be completely satisfied by the testimony of the saints. He is not even disturbed by the fact that saints flourish most happily within that rigid framework of Catholic dogma that he so wholeheartedly despises.

The witness of the saints is supplemented by the testimony of all those who have felt the need to worship and who have gratified that need. If the religious appetite, the craving for worship, which is one of the most ancient and most universal of human instincts, does not correspond to some objective reality, it is the only human appetite that feeds on complete illusion. It is, indeed, characteristic of this muddle-headed age that the consolation that religion affords should be used as an argument against the objective reality of religion. This is much as if one were to argue that cows do not exist because beef is so consoling to a hungry man. Nor is the religious appeal to the consensus of all mankind refuted by the fact that various false beliefs have been universally held at different periods of human history. It is invalid to argue that because all men were mistaken in believing the earth to be flat, all saints may be mistaken in believing that God exists, for there is a vital distinction between theories about the physical universe and facts of spiritual experience. Only experts can verify or disprove the former, whereas the latter are tested daily by ordinary people in the normal course of life. The theory, for instance, that the earth was flat was accepted lightly and without examination because it had no relevance to the practical problems of life and was consequently never put to the test of experience. And this theory was abandoned as lightly as it had been held, when the experts decided against it. But the belief in the existence of God, which, if strongly held, has the most profound effect upon life, and has some effect even if lightly held, has stood the test of experience in every age and in every race. We may well despair of the possibility of arriving at truth by human testimony if we sweep aside as a collective hallucination the common experience of the mystics of every religion, of every race, and of every century.

It is illegitimate for the individual to appeal to his own individual religious experience when arguing with a man who has enjoyed no religious experience whatever. But just as blind men might deduce the reality of art from the consensus of art lovers, so those who are religiously blind may deduce from the consensus of the mystics the reality of the supernatural world. It is, indeed, impossible to remain unimpressed by the verdict of the mystics on the points on which they all agree. Now, the mystics are at one in their assertion that no happiness compares with the happiness of those who have established communion with God. Sensuality and self-indulgence may be compared to the dirt darkening a window, for the divine rays, so the mystics assert, cannot reach the soul unless the window has been cleansed by asceticism.

"It will be found," writes Dean Inge in his *Lectures on Christian Mysticism*,

> that men of pre-eminent saintliness agree very closely in what they tell us. They tell us that they have arrived at an unshakable conviction, not based on inference but on immediate experience, that God is a spirit with whom the human spirit can hold intercourse; that in Him meet all that they can imagine of goodness, truth and beauty; that they can see His footprints everywhere in Nature, and feel His presence within them as the very life of their life, so that in proportion as they come to themselves they come to Him. They tell us what separates us from Him and from happiness is, first, self-seeking in all its forms; and, secondly, sensuality in all its forms; that these are the ways of darkness and death which hide from us the face of God; while the path of the just is like a shining light which shineth more and more until the perfect day.[29]

The saint, then, is a signpost pointing to the supernatural, a dramatic reminder not only of the existence of God but also of our obligations to God. The very extravagances of the saints are necessary to startle us out of our complacent self-satisfaction. Indeed, their extravagant preoccupation with the next world may be necessary to compensate for our no-less-exaggerated preoccupation with this world.

The most fantastic exaggerations of the saints at least serve to remind us of those Christian standards that we are only too ready to forget. We who find it impossible to love and difficult to be kind to our neighbor need to be startled into penitence by

[29] Dean Inge, *Lectures on Christian Mysticism* (1899), 326.

such acts of staggering love as the loving embrace with which St. Francis welcomed the leper. It is indeed in such glorious super-fluities of devotion that the saint shows the full royalty of a love that can rise superior to the movements of the flesh because it is transformed by the power *ejus divinitatis qui humanitatis nostrae fieri dignatus est particeps.*

These excesses of charity may be, as William James insists, a creative force. The love that the saint lavishes on the unlovable has many a time worked miracles. The world indeed would be a dreary place if there were "no one ready to be duped many a time rather than live always on suspicion; no one glad to treat individuals pas-sionately and impulsively rather than by general rules of prudence.... We can never be sure in advance of any man that his salvation by the way of love is hopeless." And William James continues: "Saints are the animators of potentialities of goodness which, but for them, would lie for ever dormant. It is not possible to be quite as mean as we naturally are when they have passed before us. One fire kindles another; and without that over-trust in human worth which they show, the rest of us would lie in spiritual stagnancy."

The saint is a living reminder of a truth that the modern world has forgotten. His life is an argument for the importance of being holy. The world of today is in desperate need of saints to coun-teract that reversal of values that began with the Renaissance. The medieval world believed that learning was important, but that piety was still more important. The modern world regards piety as faintly ridiculous and education as the panacea for all evils. Outlines of Science and Outlines of Modern Knowledge sell by tens of thousands. Few publishers would risk any money on an Outline of Piety.

It should be unnecessary to insist that learning was honored in the Middle Ages. Huxley paid a great but by no means an undeserved compliment to the medieval universities when he wrote, "I doubt if the curriculum of any modern university shows so clear and generous a comprehension of what is meant by culture, as this old Trivium and Quadrivium does."

Education is important; art is important; science is important; but these things are only means to an end. "All evil," as St. Thomas Aquinas says, "is the mistaking of means for ends." This, indeed, was the fundamental error of the Renaissance, for the leaders of the Renaissance worshipped art, science, and physical beauty as ends in themselves. "What is art," as Samuel Butler remarked, "that it should have a sake?"

And with this reversal of values went another change. The humility of the Christian gave place to the pride of the humanist.

The Renaissance reversal of values is the theme of the most Catholic-minded book ever written by a non-Catholic, *The Stones of Venice*. Ruskin hated the Renaissance. He was not fair to the Renaissance — prophets never are fair — but he was more than justified in his conviction that the spirit of the Renaissance was the spirit of pagan pride, the Renaissance of a humanism that denied the supernatural, that worshipped the intellect and despised the soul. It is his reaction against the Renaissance that is the inspiration of passages such as these:

> Therefore with respect to knowledge, we are to reason and act exactly as with respect to food. We no more live to know than we live to eat. We live to contemplate, enjoy, act, adore; and we may know all that is to be known in this world and what Satan knows in the other without being able to do any of that.

Elsewhere he writes:

And so observe, the first important consequence of our fully understanding this pre-eminence of the soul will be the due understanding of that subordination of knowledge respecting which so much has already been said. For it must be felt at once that the increase of knowledge, merely as such, does not make the soul larger or smaller; that in the sight of God, all the knowledge man can gain is as nothing; but that the soul, for which the great scheme of Redemption was laid, be it ignorant or be it wise, is all in all: and in the activity, strength, health and well-being of the soul, lies the main difference, in this life, between one man and another.

All of which must make sad reading for the sort of people who believe that men may be graded in accordance with the number of facts that they have contrived to memorize before, during, and after their university career. Ruskin's protest against the servile worship of learning, against the idolatry of science, and against the accumulation of knowledge as an end in itself made no impression on his contemporaries. And perhaps the ineffectiveness of much that passes for religion in the modern world is due not a little to the fact that so many ministers of religion unconsciously accept the Renaissance scheme of values.

A well-known American Methodist has kindly sent me a copy of his book called *Can I Know God?* The answer would seem to be, "Yes, if I graduate at a modern, progressive university." Gratitude to the God who provides us with university extension lectures finds expression in the following *Te Deum:*

Our Father, bring us into the highest harmony within our own lives. What a universe Thou has given us! What revealing things we have here on our campus! What scholarship! What telescopes! What microscopes! What revealing things! Who of all people in the world ought to find their way? We! Circumstances like these bring us to the height of living. Bind our lives to each other and lead us to our rightful home with Thee. In Jesus' name we ask it. Amen.

To become a Catholic is to pass from the world that reveres brains, and hates and despises holiness, to a world that respects brains and reveres sanctity. Even in the eyes of a bad Catholic, the Curé d'Ars takes precedence of all the kings of the earth, for he is the peer of St. Augustine, St. Francis, and St. Teresa. The Catholic honors genius, but whereas he bows to Newton, he kneels to the Curé d'Ars.

"The Kingdom of Heaven," wrote Matt Talbot, a Dublin working man of great sanctity, "was promised not to the sensible or to the educated, but to such as have the spirit of little children." A hard saying, which our Victorian grandfathers professed to accept but which the modern world more honestly rejects with scorn. A hard saying and a touchstone to discriminate between the real and the nominal Catholic. For unless a man is prepared to bank with complete conviction on the Catholic scale of values, unless he puts piety first and cleverness second, he has been infected to a greater or lesser degree by the heresy of humanism. Piety is the touchstone, and in his attitude to piety, we discover the Catholic-minded man.

Four young people recently went to the cinema. The play opened with High Mass. The hero goes to the war and is reported killed. The heroine enters a convent and takes her final vows.

Of the four people watching this play, one was a young man who had recently been received into the Church, another was a young woman who had not been to Mass or Confession for two years. The other two were non-Catholics. The film made an instant appeal both to the convert and to the lapsed Catholic. The young woman who had given up practicing her religion followed with sympathetic anxiety the conflict between natural and supernatural love. Though she herself was cheerfully living in a state of mortal sin, she accepted as self-evident the main theme of the play, that the severance of two ardent lovers was a lesser tragedy than the infidelity of a nun to her vows. The other two members of the party thought the play very silly and were outraged by the nun's fantastic sacrifice.

Saints—and this is not the least of the services that they render to their fellow men—keep alive a deep respect for piety even among the impious.

St. Peter Claver, as we have seen, was out of sympathy with the spirit of his age, as expressed in the Renaissance movement, which was changing the mind of the Europe in which he had been born.

In his youth, his scholarship had attracted the attention of his superiors, but he never pursued his studies nor attempted to impart to others the secular knowledge that he had acquired. It was not the ignorance of the uneducated but the ignorance of the unbaptized that distressed him. He devoted himself to the instruction of the slaves, but the instruction was not on modern lines, for he instructed them in Christian doctrine and in Christian practice, but in nothing else.

St. Peter Claver followed his vocation, and there are many vocations, of which the teaching profession is not the least noble. It would be a disaster if all Catholics were as sublimely indifferent to the importance of secular education as was Fr. Claver, but it would be even more disastrous if the ideals of Catholic education were infected by the anti-Catholic atmosphere in which we live, and if Catholics, in consequence, ceased to act with complete conviction on the belief that the primary object of education must be to make men better Christians.

We have here no question of competing alternatives. "Seek ye first the kingdom of God, and his righteousness; and all these things shall be added unto you" (Matt. 6:33). The issue between the Catholics and their opponents is not whether "all these things" are desirable, but whether "the Kingdom of God and his righteousness" should be our supreme concern. A question, therefore, rather of precedence than of competition.

St. Peter Claver, as we have seen, acted on the principle of concentrating exclusively on the Kingdom of God, not caring whether "all these things" were added or not. But here, as in so many other matters, the saint, by his emphasis on truths that are in danger of being obscured, tends to compensate for the dereliction of less heroic Christians, and we who live in a society servile in its worship of cleverness have much to learn from a saint who never faltered in his belief that the wisdom of this world is foolishness with God.

Sophia Institute

Sophia Institute is a nonprofit institution that seeks to nurture the spiritual, moral, and cultural life of souls and to spread the gospel of Christ in conformity with the authentic teachings of the Roman Catholic Church.

Sophia Institute Press fulfills this mission by offering translations, reprints, and new publications that afford readers a rich source of the enduring wisdom of mankind.

Sophia Institute also operates the popular online resource CatholicExchange.com. *Catholic Exchange* provides world news from a Catholic perspective as well as daily devotionals and articles that will help readers to grow in holiness and live a life consistent with the teachings of the Church.

In 2013, Sophia Institute launched Sophia Institute for Teachers to renew and rebuild Catholic culture through service to Catholic education. With the goal of nurturing the spiritual, moral, and cultural life of souls, and an abiding respect for the role and work of teachers, we strive to provide materials and programs that are at once enlightening to the mind and ennobling to the heart; faithful and complete, as well as useful and practical.

Sophia Institute gratefully recognizes the Solidarity Association for preserving and encouraging the growth of our apostolate over the course of many years. Without their generous and timely support, this book would not be in your hands.

www.SophiaInstitute.com
www.CatholicExchange.com
www.SophiaInstituteforTeachers.org